THE BATTLE

—— OF ——

FORT DONELSON

No Terms but Unconditional Surrender

JAMES R. KNIGHT

Series Editor Douglas Bostick

Charleston · London

THE
History
PRESS

Published by The History Press
Charleston, SC 29403
www.historypress.net

Copyright © 2011 by James R. Knight
All rights reserved

First published 2011

Manufactured in the United States

ISBN 978.1.60949.129.1

Library of Congress Cataloging-in-Publication Data

Knight, James R., 1945-
The Battle of Fort Donelson : no terms but unconditional surrender / James R. Knight.
p. cm.
Includes bibliographical references and index.
ISBN 978-1-60949-129-1
1. Fort Donelson, Battle of, Tenn., 1862. I. Title.
E472.97.K58 2011
973.7'31--dc22
2011000843

Contents

Contents

Acknowledgements and a Note on Sources

The Civil War was the watershed event in our early history as a nation and, as such, has been subjected to the scrutiny of some of the best minds of the last century and a half. The fact that even now, almost 150 years on, new information and fresh perspectives are constantly coming forward is testimony to the abiding interest and complexity of the subject.

In this brief overview of the first major campaign of the war, I function more as a storyteller than a historian, using the work of a number of top-notch scholars to recast the story and relate it to a new audience who may be taking a serious look at the subject for the first time during this upcoming sesquicentennial.

Where possible, I have relied on the Official Records and the Naval Supplement (listed in Bibliography) for facts, reports from various participants and orders to and from the various commanders and units, but it would have been impossible to piece together this complex campaign without the work of several excellent historians, as well as others who have been a great help. For the details of the overall campaign, Kendal D. Gott's *Where the South Lost the War* and Benjamin Franklin Cooling's *Forts Henry and Donelson: The Key to the Confederate Heartland* were absolutely essential, and they are cited many times in this work. Additionally, there are passages that represent my own efforts to consolidate information from several different sources and retell it in a new way. It should be understood that even if they are not specifically cited in such passages, those two authors were almost always contributors in some way to my basic understanding of the story, and this book owes them a great deal.

For insight on major participants, Jack Hurst's *Men of Fire* is an excellent study of the early careers of Ulysses S. Grant and Nathan Bedford Forrest, along with Grant's own memoirs and a recent biography by Geoffrey Perret. Additional information on Forrest is from Jordan and Pryor's *The Campaigns of General Nathan Bedford Forrest*, first published in 1868. For information on Albert Sidney Johnston, see Charles P. Roland's *Soldier of Three Republics*. As always, David R. Logsdon's *Eyewitnesses* series provided a wealth of firsthand accounts and quotations.

As all military historians understand, no amount of research can take the place of actually walking the ground. For this, I'm grateful to Jim Jobe, the National Park Service ranger at Fort Donelson National Battlefield who took several hours out of his day to show me the story from the level of the farm boys in Blue and Gray. To top things off, as we stood at the Lower Water Battery, one of the park's bald eagles flew past us up the Cumberland River. Just that experience was worth the trip.

Finally, thanks to the great folks at The History Press for giving me the chance to tell this fascinating story and for all of the support, as usual. An old retired history geek couldn't ask for more.

Prologue

CAIRO, ILLINOIS: FEBRUARY 2, 1862

As the month of February in 1862 began in this bustling river town at the confluence of the Ohio and Mississippi Rivers, the conflict between the North and the South had been a shooting war now for almost ten months. In the beginning, President Abraham Lincoln and his government hoped that the "rebellion" could be put down in short order and asked for volunteers to serve the standard militia commitment of ninety days, but things hadn't gone too well.

On July 21, 1861, at Manassas, Virginia, a "green" Southern army had sent General Irvin McDowell and his equally green Federal troops running back to Washington in panic, along with several members of Congress and other spectators. Three weeks later, in Missouri, Federal troops under General Nathaniel Lyon were beaten by the Confederate Missouri State Guard under Sterling Price, and Lyon was killed, making him the first Federal general officer to be claimed by the war. In November 1861, there had been a small fight at Belmont, Missouri, but it had to be called a draw at best. So far in the war, in spite of its superiority in resources of almost every kind, the Federal army had, for the most part, been beaten on the battlefield, but an almost unknown brigadier general with his headquarters in this river town was determined to change that, at least here in the West.

If you had been looking for a war hero from central casting, the Federal commander at Cairo would probably never have been considered. At five feet, eight inches and 135 pounds, this thirty-nine-year-old man with a short, slightly scruffy beard could have blended into any crowd, but in his case looks were deceiving. He was actually a West Point graduate and a combat veteran who had been twice promoted for bravery in the Mexican-American War. In 1854, however, he had resigned from the army under something of a cloud, and for the next seven years he struggled to make a living in the civilian world, without much success. In April 1861, he was working in his father's leather goods business in Galena, Illinois, when the war came and changed his life forever.

Early on, because of his West Point background, he was asked to enroll a new regiment. Eventually, the governor appointed him to lead it, with the rank of colonel, and soon after, with the help of a friendly congressman, he was made a brigadier general of Illinois Volunteers. He was as surprised as anyone at his promotion, having first read about it in a newspaper.

Such are the quirks of history that a man who had taken eleven years in the regular army to rise to the rank of captain had, in just over nine months, gone from being a civilian clerk in his father's store to a general officer and the commander of more troops than had made up the entire United States Army less than a year before. He was also now preparing to lead the Federal army's first major campaign against the Confederacy. The early sparring matches were over. North America's greatest conflict was about to begin in deadly earnest.

Bowling Green, Kentucky: February 2, 1862

On this same Sunday morning, 150 miles to the east, the commander of the Confederate Department of the West went about his duties. In almost every way, he was the opposite of the obscure brigadier from Illinois with whom his fate was now linked. At six feet, one inch and still trim after West Point and thirty-five years in the "Old Army," he was resplendent in his dress uniform and looked every inch a soldier. He was the highest-ranking Confederate officer in the field and was, by all accounts, at the height of his powers and the pinnacle of his career. Today was his fifty-ninth birthday, but it might have been happier if the tactical position of his command had been better.

He had been in California when the war broke out, and it had taken him until September to make the overland trek back to Virginia to offer his services to the Confederacy. President Jefferson Davis, his old friend and West Point underclassman, had welcomed him with open arms, later saying that he considered him "the greatest soldier, the ablest man, civil or military, Confederate or Federal, then living."[1] It was no surprise, then, that he was given command of the enormous Department of the West, which stretched from the Cumberland Gap to the Mississippi River, on across Arkansas to Indian Territory and points west. On this February morning, however, his main concern was the more than four-hundred-mile-long Tennessee/Kentucky border.

When he arrived in Nashville in early September 1861, it didn't take the new Confederate commander long to realize the enormity of his problem. At the beginning of the war, each Southern state raised its own militia that was commanded by its own officers and armed with whatever was available. Only recently had those troops been moved from state control into the Confederate army. The new commander found himself with many officers of questionable ability and many troops who had little or no formal training and who were armed with whatever muskets or shotguns they had brought from home—in some cases with nothing at all. In this, however, he was not alone. Some of his counterparts in the North were facing the same problems.

Given the situation the new Confederate commander found when he arrived in Nashville, his best defense, while he struggled to organize his department, was deception. In order to buy some time, he began a campaign of disinformation designed to convince his opposite numbers north of the Ohio River that his strength was much more impressive than it really was and that his intention was to attack them at the earliest opportunity. Fortunately for the Confederate cause, many of the Federal commanders were more than willing to believe the worst. As more rumors of Confederate troop buildups came in, Federal commanders in places like Cincinnati and Louisville, who were dealing with their own headaches of supply and organization, spent much more time and energy planning the defenses of their own territory than they did in planning offensive moves against the South. This had managed to give the Confederate commander about five months to pull something together, but that grace period was now over.

In early January, at the urging of President Lincoln, the Federal commander at Louisville finally sent a thrust southeast toward the Cumberland Gap and east Tennessee. The small Confederate army in that area had met the Federal forces two weeks ago at Mill Springs, Kentucky, and been routed. Nothing but the desolation of the countryside kept the Federal army from pushing on to Knoxville or even to the outskirts of Nashville itself. It was only due to the wilderness of southeast Kentucky that the Confederate right flank had not been turned already, and now, on his birthday, the Confederate commander waited for the proverbial other shoe to drop, not knowing that things were already underway.

This, then, was the situation in the most crucial part of what became known as the Western Theater of the Civil War. An almost unknown Federal brigadier general was moving to threaten the defensive line of the nationally famous and respected senior field commander of the Confederate army who was now off balance and vulnerable. Such are the fortunes of war that, in three weeks, the Federal brigadier general would be a national hero, with his name on the front page of every newspaper in the North. In two years, he would command the entire Federal army. In seven years, he would be the president of the United States. In spite of the incredible destruction and carnage that he would be a part of, the Civil War was the best thing that ever happened to the career of Ulysses S. Grant.

As for the famous Confederate commander, by the end of March, he had retreated along more than 250 miles of bad roads and conceded all of Kentucky and most of middle Tennessee to the enemy. Sixty-three days after this, his fifty-ninth birthday, General Albert Sidney Johnston would bleed to death on the battlefield for lack of a simple tourniquet. Johnston would fall at the edge of a peach orchard near a little Methodist church called Shiloh Meetinghouse while trying to redeem his reputation and recapture some of the ground he had lost. On that day, April 6, 1862, he became—as he remains today—the highest-ranking American soldier ever killed in combat.

The Federal campaign against the two Confederate forts guarding the Tennessee and Cumberland Rivers, as they flowed out of Tennessee into Kentucky, resulted in the South's first major defeat of the Civil War, as well as, at least in the Western Theater, the one from which it never fully recovered.[2]

I suppose it could be said that the seeds of our Civil War were sown with the adoption of our Constitution in 1787. The codifying of the institution of slavery in the Constitution, along with the provision to count slaves as three-fifths of a person for purposes of representation, was a concession to the Southern states necessary to ensure the adoption of the Constitution at all, but it was seen by many as a time bomb. A slaveholder himself, Thomas Jefferson made a prophetic statement while contemplating the situation that, more than a hundred years after his death, was carved on his memorial in Washington: "Indeed I tremble for my country when I reflect that God is just, that his justice cannot sleep forever."

As Jefferson foresaw, slavery was a problem that would not go away. By the 1830s, England had abolished the practice in its empire, and a quite vocal abolition movement had sprung up in America. Over the next thirty years, the nation divided itself more and more, politically, economically and socially, into two entities—one free and one slave. With the election of 1860, the division was complete. Lincoln won with less than 40 percent of the popular vote, and he received not a single electoral vote from any of the states that would later form the Confederacy or from any of the Border States that would play such an important role in the war in the West.

When war finally did come, in April 1861, many in the North saw it as the fulfillment of Jefferson's fears for his country, while many in the South saw it as the Second American Revolution. One thing, however, they both had in common—when the war finally came, neither side was ready.

Chapter 1

The Confederates

April to September 1861

S oon after the election of Abraham Lincoln became official, South Carolina led off the secession of the states that would become the Confederacy by its vote in December 1860; within about six weeks, it had been joined by six others. These states then met in Montgomery, Alabama, in early February 1861 and formed the Confederate States of America, but Tennessee was not among them. Governor Isham Harris was a supporter of the Confederacy, and he had proposed that a convention be held in the state to consider the question of secession, but the voters rejected it. Tennessee, then as now, was divided into three regions. West Tennessee was heavily sympathetic to the Confederate cause, while east Tennessee was heavily pro-Union. It was the crucial middle Tennessee area that tipped the balance against separation when it was first purposed.

The number of Confederate states stood at seven until the second week in April, when the United States Navy attempted to resupply Fort Sumter in Charleston Harbor and South Carolina troops opened fire. The opening of hostilities, plus Lincoln's call to each state for troops to put down the rebellion, changed many minds all across the South. In neighboring Kentucky, where loyalties were just as divided as in Tennessee, Governor Magoffin refused to furnish any troops to the Federal government for what he called a "wicked purpose." Likewise, many Tennesseans who had not been prepared to leave the Union in February could not abide the thought of sending Tennessee troops to answer Lincoln's call, knowing that those troops would be used against their fellow Southerners. Governor Harris said that he would not furnish a single man for coercion but would raise fifty thousand for the defense of "our rights and those of our Southern brethren."[3] When Harris then called a second time for a vote on secession, he got a much more favorable reception. This time, the proposition passed, and a call for volunteers went out. By the time Tennessee's secession became official, on June 8, 1861, three more states had seceded as well, making Tennessee the last of the eleven states to join the Southern Confederacy.

Raising troops for the defense of the state was not a problem—men came forward in great numbers—but arming them and outfitting them for war were different matters. At the beginning of the war, Tennessee had on hand just over ten thousand small arms of all kinds and only four pieces of artillery, two of which were out of commission. Even that inadequate number was misleading. Of the rifles and muskets, fewer than two thousand were of the modern percussion type, the rest being antiquated flintlocks, of which almost half were classified as unserviceable. Some militia companies were already armed, and many men had brought a shotgun or squirrel rifle from home, but many recruits still had to be turned away for lack of available arms.[4] So critical was the small arms situation that over eight months later some of the Tennessee troops in the first major battle on state soil would carry those War of 1812–era flintlocks into battle.

To bring order to the flurry of recruitment, Governor Harris called on a politically powerful lawyer named Gideon J. Pillow. In spite of having no formal military training, Pillow had been appointed a general officer in the Mexican-American War, largely on the strength of his being a law partner of President James K. Polk. Pillow's reputation coming out of the Mexican-American War was decidedly mixed. No one denied his energy or his personal bravery on the field, but he could be abrasive in his relations with other officers and erratic and shortsighted in his decision making. Pillow also did not get along especially well with his commander, General Winfield Scott, who considered the political appointee to be insubordinate. Pillow later returned the favor by writing extensively against General Scott when he was considering running for president.[5]

By the beginning of the war, Pillow, in spite of his considerable political clout in Tennessee, had no shortage of detractors. Even so, no one could deny that he had an enthusiasm and personal magnetism that could inspire troops to follow him. Commissioned a major general of the state's forces, he set up his headquarters in Memphis and began to organize the Provisional Army of Tennessee. Such was Pillow's energy and talent for organization— and such was the overwhelming response to the governor's call for troops and additional arms—that when Tennessee officially left the Union in

Major General
Leonidas Polk, friend
of Jefferson Davis,
West Point graduate
with no military
experience and
Episcopal bishop.
First commander
of the Department
of the West and
later commander of
Confederate forces at
Columbus, Kentucky.
*Courtesy of the Library
of Congress.*

early June 1861, it already had several camps of instruction in operation and twenty-four infantry regiments, some artillery units and one cavalry regiment available for service.[6]

In addition to mustering troops, Governor Harris also began taking other steps for the defense of his state. Since it was obvious to anyone who could read a map that control of the Tennessee and Cumberland Rivers would be vital to the security of Tennessee and, by extension, to the security of the Confederacy as a whole, the governor began to address this issue even before the state officially left the Union. That job went to Daniel S. Donelson.

A lawyer by trade, Donelson was commissioned a brigadier general and tasked with forming a group to select likely sites for fortifications that would control both rivers. Since Kentucky had declared itself "neutral" in the conflict, these sites had to be on the Tennessee side of the border, which eliminated some promising locations. By mid-May, a site just downstream from the village of Dover had been selected for the Cumberland River. It was on some bluffs about a hundred feet above the river and was well suited for the job. A mile or so away, the town of Dover had a steamboat landing and road connections back to Nashville. It was approved and named, naturally enough, Fort Donelson. The Tennessee River at this point was only twelve miles to the west, as the crow flies, but finding a suitable site there would prove more of a problem.

Placing the two forts roughly opposite each other and only a dozen miles apart had great military advantages, so the east bank of the Tennessee River was the only place seriously considered. Unfortunately, it was low and swampy, and the sites that offered anything like the elevation of the high ground at Fort Donelson were too far north—across the Kentucky line. Major William F. Foster of the First Tennessee Infantry and a civil engineer named Adna Anderson had laid out Fort Donelson and now selected a site on the Tennessee at the mouth of Standing Rock Creek that they believed was above the high-water marks in the area. General Donelson, however, had made his own tour of the area and had selected a site a few miles farther north at Kirkman's Old Landing.

Foster and Anderson strongly objected to Donelson's site, citing the low ground and the dominating bluffs across the river that, in enemy hands, would render the fort largely defenseless. Donelson evidently believed that the site's clear view of the river for several miles outweighed its faults in other areas. Finally, the head of the Tennessee Corps of Engineers was called in to make the final decision. His name was Bushrod Johnson, and he sided with General Donelson. Within a few months, everyone involved would come to regret that decision.

The Tennessee River site was named for Senator Gustavus A. Henry, and work began at the two sites right away. Fort Henry was able to mount and test-fire its first gun by the middle of July, but then work slowed to a crawl on both rivers as most of the resources of men and artillery were shifted westward to sites on the Mississippi.[7]

Once Tennessee entered the Confederacy, Gideon Pillow assumed that he would lead the state's troops he had organized, but in early July, he found that he was mistaken. Word came from Richmond that President Davis had created the Confederate Department of the West and that a major general was coming to Memphis to transfer Tennessee's Provisional Army into Confederate service, leaving Pillow a general without a command. That major general was Leonidas Polk, a member of one of middle Tennessee's most prominent families and a second cousin to the late president James K. Polk, Pillow's former law partner.

In spite of being a West Point graduate, Leonidas Polk had no real military experience. His appointment was partly a product of the search for West Pointers to fill senior positions, whatever their real qualifications, and partly because he was an old friend of President Davis's, having graduated a year ahead of him at the academy in 1827. Within a year, Polk had resigned his commission to attend a seminary; now, more than thirty years later, he was an Episcopal bishop. Until his death in 1864, Polk managed to fulfill both roles—commanding troops during the week and leading worship services in the field on Sundays.

With Polk's appointment, Gideon Pillow began a campaign to have his own state commission as a major general converted into a Confederate one, but this was delayed by President Davis, himself an old Mexican-American War veteran who knew Gideon Pillow's reputation quite well. Eventually, Pillow was given a Confederate commission, but only as a brigadier general, to serve under Polk's command in west Tennessee. Pillow took this as something of an insult, which only confirmed his disdain for West Point–type professional soldiers who, he correctly believed, looked down on him.

Polk and Pillow would prove to be an unfortunate team—the bishop, unsure of himself out of his vestments after so many years and back in uniform, was easily influenced by Pillow, his more dynamic, aggressive and politically ambitious new subordinate. Within two months, they would take matters along the Mississippi into their own hands, with far-reaching implications for the defense of Tennessee.

Chapter 2

The Federals

April to September 1861

Be careful Ulysses, you're a general now. It's a good job. Don't lose it.
—Jesse R. Grant to his son Ulysses, August 1861

A long the north bank of the Ohio River in the spring and early summer of 1861, much the same sort of frantic activity was going on—with many of the same problems that former brothers in Tennessee and those all across the South were having. President Lincoln's call for volunteers after Fort Sumter was answered enthusiastically by the midwesterners with much the same result—searches were made for experienced military men to enroll and make some sort of soldiers out of the Ohio, Indiana, Illinois and Iowa farm boys, and men were turned away for lack of arms and equipment. One thing the Northerners did not have to contend with was the bitter debate over loyalty that went on in Tennessee before secession and was still going on in Kentucky, which had decided to declare itself neutral and deny the use of the state to the forces of either side. That's not to say that the passion for the Union was universal in the states north of the Ohio by any means. In the southern parts of the states of Ohio, Indiana and Illinois, there were many who had strong family and economic ties across the river, and significant groups of Confederate sympathizers remained active in all three states through most of the war.

Into this swirl of activity and intense political intrigue stepped Ulysses S. Grant, intent on getting a command in the Union army that first summer of the war. While politicians and their friends were being given commands left and right without a day of military experience, the man who would become the Union's most famous soldier was neglected. Nothing seemed to come easy, but Grant was persistent and eventually got his regiment. It was this determination that many, including President Lincoln, saw later in the war. No matter what happened on the battlefield, Grant simply never, ever quit.

For the first seventeen years of his life, he was Hirum Ulysses Grant, firstborn son of Jesse and Hannah Simpson Grant of Georgetown, Ohio, but during the appointment procedure for West Point—which his father had arranged against young Ulysses' wishes—something changed. In May 1839, when he attempted to register with the adjutant at West Point under his given name, he found that the official appointment paperwork, submitted by the representative from his district, had dispensed with Hirum altogether and renamed him Ulysses S. Grant. If he wished to attend West Point, it would be under that name or not at all. Four years later, his second lieutenant's commission was made out to "Ulysses S. Grant." Since he had never liked Hirum much anyway, Grant bowed to the army and, for the rest of his life, embraced his new name, given to him by a clerical error in a congressman's office.

After graduation, even though he was the finest horseman at West Point, Lieutenant Grant was assigned to the Fourth Infantry Regiment at Jefferson Barracks, just south of St. Louis. Because of his skill with horses, Grant had hoped for a posting with the dragoons, but Jefferson Barracks had its advantages, the main one being that his West Point roommate, Frederick Dent, lived nearby. In time, Grant became a regular visitor at the Dent home and, in 1844, began to court Fred Dent's sister, Julia. By the time Grant and the Fourth Regiment moved south from St. Louis later that year, he and Julia Dent were secretly engaged, but due to the intervening Mexican-American War, it would be four years before they married.

For a boy who resisted going to West Point, when the Mexican-American War began, Grant found that he was in his element. An excellent junior officer, he was twice cited for bravery and returned to St. Louis for his marriage in 1848 as a brevet captain (a brevet was a temporary promotion, often given for bravery in combat, which may or may not become permanent). The next four years in the small peacetime army were tedious at best for the new couple, and then, in 1852, the Fourth Regiment got orders to move to California. That summer, Grant went to the West Coast alone, leaving Julia, who was expecting their second child, and their two-year-old son Fred with family.

For Brevet Captain Grant, California of 1852 (although he came to like the country) was not the promised land. Alone and half a continent away from his family, and faced with contentious superiors and a hostile wilderness, it began to seem more like purgatory. He began to treat the loneliness and despair more and more often with alcohol and considered leaving the army and going home. Deserved or not, stories of his problems with liquor would follow Grant for the rest of his life.

By the spring of 1854, he had made up his mind but was waiting for one last thing: his promotion to permanent captain. The paperwork finally reached him in early April, making him one of only five out of thirty-nine members of his West Point class to have achieved that rank. He immediately sat down and wrote two letters—one accepting the promotion and another resigning from the army. After eleven years as a soldier, Ulysses S. Grant was a civilian again. Grant wasn't the only soldier leaving the army to try his luck in the civilian world that year. Several other men left as well, but almost all of them would meet again in a few years on the battlefields of the Civil War as senior commanders—both Confederate and Federal.[8]

One thing that seemed to plague Ulysses S. Grant to the end of his life was money troubles, and on his trip home from California, he ran out of cash in New York City. Fortunately, an old friend from West Point was stationed nearby and came to his rescue. Captain Simon Bolivar Buckner assured the hotel where Grant was staying that he would be good for the bill until Grant's father could send some money so that his son could finish the trip home. Eight years later, Grant and Buckner would meet again in less cordial circumstances, and this time it would be Grant in a position to help his friend.

For the next six years, Grant tried several things, from farming to real estate sales, to make a living in the civilian world, without much success. By the spring of 1861, he had moved his family to Galena, Illinois, where he joined his brothers Simpson and Orvil in running the family leather goods business. When the news of the fall of Fort Sumter reached Galena, a town meeting was called and several speeches were made. Grant was there, and the speech that impressed him most was the one by the young lawyer who happened to represent the Grant Leather Company, John A. Rawlins. Lincoln's call for seventy-five thousand volunteers resulted in a quota for Illinois of six regiments, and the patriots in Galena were intent on contributing a company from the town. Soon another meeting was called, and the local congressional representative, Elihu B. Washburne, saw to it that Grant was in charge. Washburne was a prominent Republican with the ear of the new president, and he would become Grant's sponsor and political "guardian angel" throughout the war.

After seven years, Ulysses S. Grant was back in the army—almost. He enrolled and trained the Galena company and even furnished the pattern for a proper uniform, which the ladies of the town promptly supplied, but he refused an offer to be their captain. Grant believed that, given the national emergency and his prior experience, he should settle for no less than a colonel's commission and command of a regiment. By the first of May, Grant had taken Galena's new company to Springfield and applied to Governor Yates for a command. Unfortunately, some other military men told Yates that Grant had something of a reputation in the Old Army, and suggestions of a drinking problem made the rounds. The governor was happy to use Grant to muster in and train other units for state service, but a regimental command would not yet be forthcoming. Grant waited through May and into June. He wrote a letter to the War Department in Washington and contacted friends in Missouri and even back in his home state of Ohio, with no results. Finally, on June 15, he received the telegram he had been waiting for—from Governor Yates back in Illinois.

Elihu B. Washburne, U.S. representative from Galena, Illinois, friend of Abraham Lincoln and Ulysses S. Grant's political protector in Washington. *Courtesy of the Library of Congress.*

Grant finally had his regiment, but it was no prize. He had mustered in the Seventh District Regiment from Mattoon, Illinois, only to see it given to another commander, who turned out to be a great stump speaker but a disaster as a soldier. By now, half the regiment had deserted, and the remainder refused to serve unless given a new commander. With the regiment falling apart, Governor Yates finally turned to Grant. The new unit of Illinois farm boys was a mess, but U.S. Grant was finally back in his element.

Twelve days after taking command, Grant's regiment was sworn into Federal service as the Twenty-first Illinois infantry. At the ceremony, two congressmen spoke, not knowing that their own careers would shortly be bound up with the slightly stooped thirty-nine-year-old colonel who sat in the audience, almost certainly bored stiff by the politicians. U.S. representatives John A. McClernand and John A. Logan would both serve under Grant in the first major battle in Tennessee, and Logan would barely escape with his life.

Sent west to the Mississippi River, Grant declined the use of the railroad

and marched the Twenty-first one hundred miles to Quincy, making twenty miles a day and beginning to turn the farm boys into soldiers. They were soon ordered over the river and spent the month of July in Missouri. Early in August, Grant discovered in a newspaper that he had been made a brigadier general. Congressman Washburne, his new political protector, had even managed to have Grant's rank backdated to May 17, a month before he was a colonel. This early in the war, those extra three months of seniority would prove quite important.

Now that he was a general, Grant began assembling a staff, and one of the first people he asked to join it was the young lawyer from Galena, John A Rawlins. He accepted

Brigadier General Ulysses S. Grant, commander of the Federal District of Cairo and leader of the campaign against the Tennessee and Cumberland River forts. *Courtesy of the Library of Congress.*

View of Cairo, Illinois, circa 1861, with barracks in the background. *From* The Photographic History of the Civil War.

Brigadier General Ulysses S. Grant and his staff. Cairo, Illinois, October 1861. *Courtesy of the Library of Congress.*

and became Grant's assistant adjutant general, with the rank of captain. For the rest of the war—indeed, for the rest of his life—Rawlins was a loyal Grant supporter and, at times, almost an alter ego—his abilities lay in areas where Grant had little interest and even less talent. Rawlins was at home dealing with the politicians, the bureaucracy and the press, and he also took on an unofficial assignment for Congressman Washburne that was vital to Grant's success, given the persistence of the rumors from his past—making sure that the general stayed sober.

The rest of the month of August was spent maneuvering without any fighting, and on September 4, Brigadier General Grant moved his headquarters to Cairo, Illinois. Three months after reentering the army, Grant now commanded a district that included southeast Missouri and southern Illinois. Within another month, he would command thirteen thousand men. He was also the officer responsible for opposing any Confederate move into western Kentucky, just across the river, and he didn't have long to wait.[9]

Chapter 3

Albert Sidney Johnston
Takes Command

*I hoped and expected that I had others who would prove generals, but I knew
I had one...*
  –Jefferson Davis on Albert Sidney Johnston[10]

I f the Union brigadier general who gave the Confederacy its first real
test in the West was almost unknown and burdened with a questionable
reputation from the Old Army, the man who now came to put in place the
defenses he would have to defeat was probably the best-known and most
respected soldier in the nation. West Point graduate in 1826, a veteran of
the Black Hawk War, a former commander of the Army of the Republic of
Texas, a veteran of the Mexican-American War, former commander of the
Second U.S. Cavalry, commander of the Utah Campaign of 1857–58 and
former commander of the Army Department of the Pacific, it's doubtful
that any man in North America had more experience actually commanding
men in battle and managing troops in the field than Albert Sidney Johnston.

When Abraham Lincoln was elected president, the Johnston family was
preparing for a long journey. Johnston was by now a brevet brigadier general
and had been given command of the new Department of the Pacific, which
united the earlier Departments of California and Oregon. Ironically, Johnston's
new command had been given to him by Secretary of War John B. Floyd, who
would shortly become Johnston's subordinate in the Confederate army and a
major figure in the battle to come. On December 21, 1860, Johnston and his
family set sail from New York via the Isthmus of Panama for San Francisco. The
day before, South Carolina had become the first state to secede from the Union.

General Albert Sidney Johnston, commander of the Department of the West and highest-ranking Confederate officer in the field. *Courtesy of the Library of Congress.*

As the Johnstons prepared for the trip, one issue had to be resolved. As befitting persons of their rank and station in the mid-nineteenth century, General Johnston and his wife, Eliza, each had a personal servant. Since California was a free state, this posed a problem, as their servants were both slaves. Eliza's maid was sold to her stepson, but Johnston's body servant, Randolph Hughes, asked to go with him. The formalities were satisfied when Johnston freed the young man and then signed him to a five-year contract at a regular salary. The trip across the isthmus was dangerous, but the Johnston family arrived in San Francisco safely by the middle of January 1861.

General Johnston would only hold his new command for about three months. Even though the trip from the East Coast to California through Panama could take almost a month for people, with the telegraph and the Pony Express to fill in the gaps, information could reach the West Coast in a few days. Johnston was able to follow the developments as his adopted home state of Texas seceded and the cold war finally became a hot one in April.

Some sources suggest that there were some Southern sympathizers in California who, knowing Johnston's Southern ties, hoped to approach him about the possibility of taking over the Federal arsenal and using the arms to begin a Confederate "revolution" in California. Having already heard the rumors, Johnston cut them short by declaring that so long as he wore the Federal uniform no government property would be touched and that any attempt on it would result in bloodshed. When Johnston did resign, all government property under his command was passed to the new commander in good order.

On April 9, 1861, Johnston received final confirmation that Texas had joined the Confederacy. That same day, he began writing his letter of resignation, not knowing that Lincoln had secretly relieved him of command more than two weeks earlier and that his replacement was already on the way. By early May, Johnston had turned over command to Brigadier General E.V. Sumner and moved his family to Los Angles to stay with Eliza's brother, Dr. John Griffin.

What happened during the next few months would become part of Albert Sidney Johnston's legend. Unable to travel by ship back to New York because of an arrest order issued by the government, Johnston, who was fifty-eight years old at the time, and a small group of Southerners crossed the Arizona and New Mexico territories on horseback in midsummer and arrived in Confederate Texas in early August. From there, Johnston hurried on to Richmond, where he met with President Davis the first week in September.

Jeff Davis and Sidney Johnston were old comrades in arms. Both native Kentuckians, they first met at Transylvania College, attended West Point together and fought together in both the Black Hawk and Mexican-American Wars. The only question in Davis's mind was where to best use his old friend. At the moment, Virginia seemed to be in good hands, with Joseph E. Johnston and P.G.T. Beauregard in charge, but the huge, sprawling Department Number Two in the West was not. General Polk, its current commander, was fully aware of his own inadequacy and had already requested that Johnston be sent to take over as department commander, and Davis agreed. Johnston was accordingly commissioned a full general—one of only five in Confederate service—and declared the ranking Confederate officer in the field, senior even to Robert E. Lee. Wasting no time, General Johnston set out for Tennessee, only to find that the strategic situation of his new command had fundamentally changed while he was in Richmond.[11]

Even though Kentucky had declared itself neutral in April and had banned the troops of either side from operating within its borders, the state was so rich in resources and so strategically vital to both the North and the South that nobody really expected that neutrality to last. Both sides had, in fact, been recruiting actively in the state and even had a few camps of instruction in operation by the time General Johnston made it across the country to Richmond. Kentuckians had even formed several units that had gone into service for both Union and Confederate armies.

Neither side wanted to be the first one to violate Kentucky's neutrality, but both sides were stretching that neutrality to the limit and were ready to pounce the moment the other made a fatal mistake. Finally, on September 3, the Confederates under Bishop Polk and Gideon Pillow made it. On September 2, in response to operations by Confederate raiders in southeast Missouri led by Jeff Thompson, Federal troops under Colonel Gustav Waagner occupied Belmont, a steamboat landing located across the Mississippi River from Columbus, Kentucky. Gideon Pillow had long coveted Columbus as the perfect site to block the river traffic, and this Federal move finally gave him the chance to convince a reluctant Leonidas Polk to go along. The next day, Pillow took Hickman, Kentucky, and by September 4 was on the bluffs at Columbus, overlooking the Mississippi, only twenty miles or so downstream from Grant's headquarters at Cairo.

With the Confederate move on Columbus, events almost seemed to take on a life of their own. Within forty-eight hours, Grant had two regiments and an artillery battery in place at Paducah, securing the mouth of the Tennessee River, and Union troops under Major General Robert Anderson and Brigadier General William T. Sherman were heading into Louisville, where they made their headquarters. The Confederate move into the state angered many Kentuckians, and the Union-dominated legislature demanded their removal, but it was too late. President Davis, who was not consulted beforehand, reluctantly sanctioned the move, since it could not be undone, and Kentucky moved more solidly into the Union camp. Three days after General Pillow entered Columbus, the Kentucky House of Representatives ordered the U.S. flag raised over the state capitol. This was the situation that confronted General Albert S. Johnston when he arrived in Nashville on September 14.

Faced with the situation as he found it upon his arrival in Nashville, Johnston made his dispositions to counter the Union moves. He had already ordered his troops in east Tennessee to move up and cover the Cumberland Gap, and on September 18, he ordered troops north from Nashville to secure Bowling Green. Johnston's line of defense now stretched from the Cumberland Gap through southern Kentucky to Bowling Green; across the Cumberland and Tennessee Rivers at Fort Donelson and Fort Henry; and on to the Mississippi River at Columbus, Kentucky. In spite of considerable raiding and probing by both sides, this line would remain in place for the next four months.

Chapter 4

Defending the Rivers

As the two sides geared up for war in early 1861, what we today would call the infrastructure for each side would be crucial to success. Much of the road system was still unsurfaced, and even on the best of them, traffic could only travel at the speed of a horse and wagon. Railroads were just coming into their own, and the advantage there went solidly to the North, which had twice the track mileage of the South and much more heavy industry to support a rail system. When it came to heavy cargoes of manufactured goods and agricultural commodities, as well as comfort and elegance of passenger travel, however, the river was still king.

West of the Appalachians, the Mississippi and Ohio and their tributaries were the arteries of commerce for the Northern states of the Midwest, as well as many of the Southern states that became the Confederacy. Near the mouth of the Mississippi, New Orleans was the largest city in the South. At the beginning of the war, a major part of midwestern agricultural and manufactured goods—and more than half of the cotton produced in the entire country—passed through its port every year. For all of these reasons and many others, control of the inland river systems of the heartland became, from the very beginning, a strategic issue of the first order for North and South alike.

For several reasons, Albert Sidney Johnston—and the Confederacy as a whole—was committed to a defensive posture. This meant that the three major rivers that ran through his department were his to protect. The loss of any one would be a major setback; the loss of all three would be little short of a catastrophe. Loss of the Mississippi would mean, among other things, loss of communication and resources from Arkansas, Texas and most of Louisiana. Loss of the Tennessee would provide the Union with a direct invasion route all the way to northern Alabama. Loss of the Cumberland would allow the Federal army to sail right into downtown Nashville.

When Johnston arrived, the Mississippi was being blockaded by Confederate troops and artillery at Columbus, Kentucky, with other installations under construction down the river toward Memphis. Closer to Nashville, Johnston was concerned about the progress of the forts guarding the Tennessee and the Cumberland. Two weeks after he took command, Johnston ordered a report on Forts Henry and Donelson from his chief engineer, Lieutenant Joseph Dixon. After his survey, Dixon reported that Fort Henry showed promise of becoming a strong position, in spite of its unfortunate location on low ground beside the river. In any case, the work was too far along to consider starting over at another site. Dixon also recommended, now that Kentucky neutrality was no longer an issue, that the high ground across the river be occupied. At Fort Donelson, Dixon found the work further behind but, again, decided that too much had been done to start over anywhere else.

In the middle of October, Major Jeremy F. Gilmer arrived and replaced Lieutenant Dixon as the chief engineer and was then put in charge of the work at both forts. Gilmer soon began his own tour of the Tennessee and Cumberland Rivers and, for the most part, agreed with Dixon's assessment but recommended that the numbers of guns at each fort be increased. Gilmer also arranged to have three barges full of stone sunk downstream from Fort Donelson to block the passage of Federal gunboats, even though people who knew the river told him that it would do no good when the winter rains came.

Johnston read Dixon's and Gilmer's reports and urged the work forward as fast as possible. He certainly realized how critical the defense of the rivers was but seemed to be satisfied to leave the work there to his subordinates. During his time as Confederate commander in the West, General Johnston never set foot at either place.[12] In fact, most of the progress that had been made by the time he arrived was mainly due to the efforts of a Prussian immigrant, a politician and a bunch of rowdy Irishmen.

Randal William McGavock was a fourth-generation American and the son of Southern aristocracy by way of the Scottish Highlands and Northern Ireland. Born into a prominent middle Tennessee family, Randal was educated at the University of Nashville and Harvard School of Law. McGavock finished his term at Harvard and returned to Nashville at about the same time as some old family friends, President James K. Polk and his wife, Sarah, were returning from Washington. The young lawyer opened an office but spent much more time on the social circuit of the Tennessee capital—attending the balls and squiring the young ladies—than he did at the courthouse. At six feet, two inches tall with a full head of red hair, he was quite the young man about town. Finally, at age twenty-nine and after several very public romances, Randal married Seraphine Derry in 1855. Three years later, he was elected mayor of Nashville with the considerable help of the large Irish community, who had adopted "Randy Mack" as one of their own.

With the coming of the war, militia companies began to form all over Tennessee, even before secession was formalized in June. In Nashville, former mayor McGavock had a built-in constituency, and by May 9 he had 124 men formed and ready. They were sworn in as Company D Tennessee Home Guard, with McGavock elected as their captain. To no one's surprise, they were Irish almost to a man. Randal's wife, "Seph," organized the Ladies Soldiers' Friend Society, and the ladies designed and made a flag for the boys to carry. It was green and featured a Gaelic harp and the words "Sons of Erin" and "Where Glory Waits You." On May 25, McGavock and his company were sent down the Cumberland to join the men already at work on what would become Fort Donelson.

Randy Mack's Irishmen may not have known much about soldiering yet, but they were well acquainted with hard labor, which was more important at this point. At Fort Donelson,

Colonel Adolphus "Uncle Dolph" Heiman, a Prussian immigrant and Mexican-American War veteran. Heiman was an architect and builder who was put in charge of the construction of Fort Henry and Fort Donelson. He was the first commander of the Tenth Tennessee "Rebel Sons of Erin." *Courtesy of the Tennessee State Library and Archives.*

they found about 350 men—mostly Irish like themselves—already at work. Commanding the work at both forts was Colonel Adolphus Heiman, a Prussian who had been in America for twenty-eight years and had served in the Mexican-American War. Trained in architecture, engineering and stonemasonry, Heiman came home from Mexico and started a construction business, building everything from public buildings to expensive private homes. Commissioned a colonel in the Tennessee Home Guard, Heiman was given the job of constructing the defenses on both rivers, which seemed to be a task that suited his considerable talents.

Colonel Heiman could be a stern taskmaster who expected a full day's work from his men, but he was a fair man who knew his business. Even though his English was so heavily accented that he was sometimes almost impossible to understand, and though he had a habit of flailing his arms and swearing loudly in German when things went wrong, the Irishmen learned to respect "Uncle Dolph," as they began to call him. When the company from Nashville arrived, Heiman formed his now 475 men into

Lieutenant Colonel Randal W. "Randy Mac" McGavock, former mayor of Nashville. McGavock organized one of the first companies of the Tenth Tennessee and was then elected lieutenant colonel of the regiment. One of the original "Rebel Sons of Erin," McGavock was killed at Raymond, Mississippi, in 1863. *Courtesy of the Tennessee State Library and Archives.*

the Tenth Tennessee Infantry Regiment of Volunteers. With the help of some political campaigning by his Nashville precinct workers, Randal McGavock won another election. He became the lieutenant colonel and second in command of the regiment. As Colonel Heiman had little interest in soldiering, he functioned more as a construction superintendent, while the military discipline and training was left to McGavock—an arrangement that worked quite well for all concerned.

By the first of July, Heiman's Tenth Tennessee Regiment had moved from Fort Donelson on the Cumberland to the Tennessee River, where Lieutenant Colonel McGavock had the same impression that everyone else had the first time they saw Fort Henry: "The fort is on the wrong side of the river!" At the time, however, Kentucky was still neutral, so they built where they were told. Reveille and roll call was at 4:00 a.m., and work often continued until sundown. The Irish lads were used to hard work, but they also kept a sharp eye out for any diversions the area might offer. Fort Henry, on the Tennessee side, was in somewhat of a wilderness, but across the river on the Kentucky side, an establishment called Peggy's Tavern provided a little patch of civilization, not to mention good Kentucky sipping whiskey. That being the case, the cross-river traffic during the boys' time off was brisk.

As a general rule, Lieutenant Colonel McGavock was fairly lenient about the nighttime excursions across the river, as long as the lads showed up reasonably sober for work the next morning, but Colonel Heiman was not so understanding. Once, when McGavock was gone, Heiman declared Kentucky off-limits and ordered the rowboats smashed. Naturally, there was a boat that survived the purge, and the lads then began to draw lots to decide who would make the whiskey run in the darkness. As the story goes, one night in August, Patrick and Timothy from Company I had the honors and made the trip over safely. On the return trip with four jugs, however, they were caught in a summer storm, and the waves rose on the Tennessee. The following conversation has come down through the years: "Bejabbers Paddy, and the boat will be overturned and we will lose our whisky!" says Tim. "We sure and we won't," answers Paddy. "We'll drink it and save it"—which they did.

Brave lads for certain. Such was the life at Fort Henry that summer. On the first of September, the Tenth Tennessee Infantry, now numbering 720 officers and men, was mustered into the Confederate army.[13]

Chapter 5

The Brown Water Navy

Although not promising quite the glory of its blue water counterpart, the strategic value of the inland river system guaranteed that the United States Navy would have to get involved early on, but it was not enthusiastic about getting entangled in a landlocked war. Within a few weeks after the war began, U.S. Navy commander John Rogers was sent west to serve as an advisor to U.S. Army general George McClellan, commander of the West at that point. His orders read in part:

> *NAVY DEPARTMENT, May 16, 1861.*
> *SIR: You will proceed to Cincinnati, Ohio, or the headquarters of General McClellan, where* [ever] *they may be, and report to that officer in regard to the expediency of establishing a naval armament on the Mississippi and Ohio rivers, or either of them, with a view of blockading or interdicting communication and interchanges with the States that are in insurrection.*

Commander Rogers reported as ordered, and McClellan immediately set him to work finding suitable craft for service on the rivers. Since the war had disrupted commerce on the Mississippi below Cairo, many boats were sitting idle and generating no revenue, and some of the owners were anxious to sell. That being the case, Rogers was soon able to make a deal for three riverboats in good condition—one, the *Lexington*, almost new. Due to the situation, Rogers was able to get the three boats for $62,000, about two-thirds of their original cost. Thinking that he had done a good job, Rogers informed his superiors at the Navy Department, only to receive a swift reprimand for exceeding his orders. It seems that the navy had no interest in raising a river flotilla, seeing that as an army problem. On June 12, Naval Secretary Welles sent Rogers a letters that said, in part:

> *The Department can not recognize or sanction any contract for boats. They are not wanted for naval purposes. If they are required for the Army, those whose business and duty it is to procure them will make requisitions on the War Department.*

Rogers had, in fact, done a good job, but he had sent the bill to the wrong place. By referring the purchase to the War Department (the army), Secretary of the Navy Gideon Welles made sure that the cost didn't come out of his budget. He was willing to provide naval armaments and possibly some crewmen, but that was all.[14]

General McClellan, of course, had been involved from the beginning, and Rogers had made the deal at his request. The army agreed to honor the contract, and work was soon begun converting the commercial steamboats into military gunboats. This involved mounting cannons and enclosing as much of the machinery as possible for protection from enemy fire. The "armor" used was actually oak planking, which would protect the crews against small arms fire, but artillery batteries were another matter. A fieldpiece of any substantial caliber could fire from shore and put a solid shot through the oak planks and reach most of the vital areas.

While the new "iron clad" gunboats would come into service a few months later, these converted boats were called "timber clads."

Commander Rogers spent the next two months overseeing the conversions and recruiting crews from among experienced river men and army units. By the middle of August, all three boats had been moved to Cairo, Illinois, where the work was finally finished; the *Lexington*, *Conestoga* and *Tyler* joined the war. Because of their vulnerability to artillery, these boats did not engage shore batteries at close range in places like Fort Henry and Fort Donelson or Columbus, Kentucky, but their armament and speed made them the masters of the rivers. They escorted the army cargo boats and transports, intercepted contraband and made raids deep into sparsely defended enemy territory.

The three converted gunboats would be a vital element in the upcoming campaign, but even as they were being finished, a whole new project was taking shape. In early August, the War Department put out bids for a new type of gunboat. This new design would be built from the keel up to cruise the sometimes shallow western rivers and be essentially an armored floating gun platform. The man who won the contract, James B. Eads of St. Louis, was a man of great experience on the Mississippi who had, by the start of the war, made a fortune building boats and salvaging wrecks and cargo. The contract reflected the harsh realities of war, and it's doubtful if any other man in the Midwest could have done it in the time allowed.

Eads was expected to deliver seven shallow-draft ironclad gunboats. They were to be 175 feet long by 51 feet wide and weigh in at more than 500 tons—122 tons of that to be the iron armor. They would require thirty-five boilers, twenty-one steam engines, 18 million feet of white oak lumber and 800 tons of iron plating and, once in operation, would burn almost 1 ton of coal an hour for a top speed of five to six knots—and they had to be ready in sixty-five days! These new "City Class" gunboats were named for towns on the rivers—*Cairo, Carondelet, Cincinnati, Louisville, Mound City, St. Louis* and *Pittsburgh*. When the first of them were officially commissioned, shortly

Flag Officer Andrew Hull Foote, commander of the navy's western flotilla. Foote supported Grant's campaign up the Tennessee and Cumberland Rivers and commanded the gunboats in the Battles of Fort Henry and Fort Donelson. *Courtesy of the Library of Congress.*

before Grant began his campaign against Fort Henry, they became the first operational ironclad warships in the Western Hemisphere. Principally designed by famous naval architect Samuel M. Pook, and having a low silhouette, they became known as "Pook's Turtles."[15]

Even though the navy first viewed the inland river theater to be an army affair, the department was willing to furnish experienced naval officers to command the boats and support the army. Accordingly, the following order was given to newly promoted navy captain Andrew Hull Foote:

> *NAVY DEPARTMENT,*
> *Washington, August 30, 1861.*
>
> *Sir: You have been selected to take command of the naval operations upon the Western waters, now organizing under the direction of the War Department. You will therefore proceed to St. Louis, Mo., with all practicable dispatch, and place yourself in communication with Major-General John C. Fremont, U.S. Army, who commands the Army of the West.*
>
> *You will cooperate fully and freely with him as to your movements… The Western movement is of the greatest importance, and the Department assigns you this duty, having full confidence in your zeal, fidelity, and judgment.*
>
> *I am, respectfully,*
> *GIDEON WELLES,*
> *Secretary of the Navy.*

Commander Rogers was asked to stay on as Foote's assistant, but he requested a transfer back to the fleet, which was eventually granted.[16]

Andrew Hull Foote was a sailor's sailor. He joined the U.S. Navy at age sixteen as a midshipman and spent eighteen of the next thirty-nine years at sea in the Atlantic, Pacific, Mediterranean and Caribbean. He was a firm believer in the temperance movement and insisted on it in all his commands. Foote's experiences commanding the USS *Perry* off the African coast, interdicting the slave trade, led to his support of the abolitionist cause and the publishing of his book titled *Africa and the American Flag* in 1859. Foote was a fighter as well as a religious man, a common combination found in many of the prominent senior officers on both sides. Foote was just as at home leading a shore party with sword in hand as he was leading Sunday services on the deck of his ship. It was said that he was equally adept at preaching, fighting or praying—whatever the situation called for.

When the war began, Foote was in charge of the Brooklyn Navy Yard. He was soon promoted to captain (the navy equivalent of an army colonel) and sent to command the flotilla of gunboats, transports, mortar boats and other craft on the western waters, as his orders above state—under the overall command of the army, of course. Foote arrived in early September just as things began to change rapidly with the end of Kentucky neutrality. The new navy commander got there just in time to watch his gunboats and transports in action, moving Grant's two regiments quickly up the Ohio to take Paducah on September 6. Before long, other naval officers like Commander Henry Walke[17] and Lieutenant Ledyard Phelps arrived to command the timber clads and support the army, while Foote labored to find the armaments and crews to outfit the new ironclad City Class boats then under construction. At the same time, James Eads had four thousand men in eight states working around the clock, trying to perform miracles in his shipyards and get the boats launched in time for the winter rains and high water on the rivers.

For the next four months, the three river steamboats—now converted to the gunboats *Tyler*, *Lexington* and *Conestoga*—supported the army and patrolled the rivers under the command of General Grant at Cairo and gave their crews invaluable experience for the coming campaign against the Tennessee and Cumberland forts. By November, they had been joined by another converted river steamer, the *New Era*, which was given some iron armor and renamed the *Essex*. When the City Class boats were commissioned in late January, the Union would have a fleet that was the absolute master of the western rivers. The few converted "Cotton Clad" boats that the Confederates could muster were completely outclassed.

Chapter 6

Command and Control

When the war became official in April 1861, both sides faced serious command and control challenges. The Confederacy had to create a military system from scratch. This, at least, gave officials the opportunity to shape such a system to fit their particular situation, if they had the foresight to do so. In the North, there was already a military establishment, which turned out to be a two-edged sword. Having a system in place was an advantage, but most of the people running that system were left over from the last war, thirteen years ago. The sheer scope of this conflict would demand a lot of new faces, and in addition to the Federal army establishment, each state had its own militia that needed officers, staff and equipment.

The defense of Tennessee passed to the Confederate government when a reluctant Leonidas Polk accepted the post of Department of the West commander in July. At that time, the entire state of Kentucky, by proclaiming itself neutral, was acting as a buffer between Polk's department and his opposite numbers north of the Ohio. In Missouri, General John C. Fremont had arrived to take command west of the Mississippi; east of the river, one of the North's rising stars was in charge.

Only thirty-four years old, this 1846 West Point graduate turned railroad executive was sought by the governors of three states to command their state militias. In the end, even though he would have preferred his home state of Pennsylvania, Governor Dennison of Ohio won the race for this gentleman's services, and he was on his way to the top. With the exception of Albert Sidney Johnston, who was directly commissioned a full general and second in seniority in the Confederate army, few men experienced a

Major General John C. Fremont, Grant's first department commander. Famous for his explorations of the West before the war, "The Pathfinder" was replaced by Major General Henry W. Halleck in November 1861. *Courtesy of the Library of Congress.*

faster rise in rank than George Brinton McClellan. On April 23, 1861, the former army captain became a major general of volunteers and commander of the Ohio Militia. Ten days later, he was mustered into Federal service and given command of the Department of Ohio, which covered three states and parts of three more. Eleven days after that, he was made a major general in the Regular Army and became the second ranking officer in the nation, behind only the aging Lieutenant General Winfield Scott, whom he would replace in six months. It was at this point that Commander John Porter arrived to be his naval advisor, and they began buying riverboats.[18]

By the end of July, McClellan was gone, called to Washington by President Lincoln after the debacle at Bull Run to build and command what would become the famous Army of the Potomac. For the next month, then, Confederate general Polk, with his headquarters in Memphis, was faced with General Fremont in St. Louis and a new commander of the Department of Ohio, General Ormsby Mitchell, in Cincinnati. Department lines were also adjusted on the Union side, with Fremont's area expanded to cover western Kentucky. The Cumberland River was now his eastern boundary.

From now until the battle for the river forts, seven months away, the Confederates would have a single commander responsible for the defense of Tennessee, while the Federal army would have two different jurisdictions opposing him, each with their own commanders and each commander with his own personal and professional agenda. In theory, at least, the Confederates had the advantage at the highest command levels of having a unified command, whereas the Federals had two different commands over the same area that didn't always work well together.

As September arrived, the war in the Tennessee/Kentucky area began to heat up, and the cast of characters began to change. By the middle of the month, Albert Sidney Johnston had arrived to replace Leonidas Polk, who was happy to now concern himself with just the western part of Tennessee and Kentucky and serve as Johnston's subordinate. Across the way, now that Kentucky was no longer neutral, a new Federal organization was forming.

Major Robert Anderson was the North's first war hero. As the commander of

General George Brinton McClellan. Promoted to command of the Federal armies in November 1861, McClellan immediately replaced both department commanders in the West. *Courtesy of the Library of Congress.*

the Federal garrison in Charleston Harbor when South Carolina seceded, Anderson had moved his men out to Fort Sumter and held out until April 13, finally surrendering after a thirty-four-hour bombardment. Anderson came back home a hero and was promoted to brigadier general. Now, four months later, he has been given the assignment to go back to his native Kentucky as the Federal commander of the new Department of the Cumberland. As Kentucky was still neutral at this point, Anderson was forced to set up shop in Cincinnati, just across the river. Anderson also brought with him as his subordinates two men who were old friends and West Point classmates.

William Tecumseh Sherman was from Ohio and an 1840 West Point graduate. Sherman was in Florida during the Seminole War but, unlike many of the Civil War senior commanders, saw no combat there or during the Mexican-American

Brigadier General Robert Anderson. Hero of Fort Sumter and first commander of the Department of Kentucky, Anderson resigned for health reasons in October 1861, leaving Brigadier General William T. Sherman in charge. *Courtesy of the Library of Congress.*

War, during which he served in California. Sherman resigned from the army in 1853 and, by 1860, was the first superintendent of the Louisiana State Seminary of Learning and Military Academy, which later became Louisiana State University. When Louisiana seceded, Sherman resigned and went back to Ohio, where his younger brother, John, a United States senator, became his brother's advocate in Washington. In July, Colonel "Cump" Sherman commanded a brigade at Bull Run and, in spite of the defeat, was commended for his performance and promoted to brigadier general. Robert Anderson had been Sherman's company commander when he was fresh out of the academy and had been a friend ever since, so when Anderson ask him to go along to Kentucky as his second in command, Sherman accepted at once. Sherman was, in fact, glad to be a subordinate at this point, telling his wife that he didn't want to command until the situation became clearer.

Another new brigadier general that Anderson asked for was George Henry Thomas, and he was something of a special case. Thomas was a native Virginian who had stayed with the Union, and as such, some questioned his loyalty. Unlike Sherman, Thomas had never left the army and had seen action in Mexico and against the Indians out West, serving under Albert S. Johnston and Robert E. Lee. Whatever others thought, Thomas's reputation in the Old Army was flawless, and Sherman, his old friend and classmate from the class of 1840, assured any who asked of Thomas's loyalty. Thomas would, in fact, prove to be one of the steadiest and most successful Federal commanders of the war if not exactly the flashiest.

Anderson and his staff were in Cincinnati by September 1 and only had a few days to wait before the Confederates violated Kentucky neutrality by taking Columbus. When Grant moved to secure Paducah and the mouth of the Tennessee, Anderson immediately moved his headquarters to Louisville, and that is where matters stood when Albert S. Johnston arrived in Nashville about ten days later.[19]

Arriving to take over his command in Nashville and finding a Federal army reported at Louisville was certainly one of the things that caused Johnston to decide to move into Kentucky himself as soon as possible. Leaving central Kentucky unoccupied was simply not an option.

Brigadier General William T. Sherman. Relieved at Louisville at his own request and replaced by Don Carlos Buell, Sherman was sent home on medical leave, being thought to be on the edge of a nervous breakdown. *Courtesy of the Library of Congress.*

Without Confederate troops to oppose them, the Federals could simply ride the Louisville & Nashville Railroad right to the border, which was only about thirty-five miles from the Tennessee capital. A Confederate advance at least as far as Bowling Green was the logical move, and Johnston found just the man to lead it waiting for him when he arrived.

Simon Bolivar Buckner was a native Kentuckian and 1844 West Point graduate. He had distinguished himself in Mexico and had been an instructor at his alma mater, but for the last six years, he had been working in the civilian world. When the Confederacy was formed, Buckner and his family were living in Louisville, and Buckner had, for the last two years, been active in the Kentucky Home Guard. With Kentucky declaring neutrality, Buckner was made a major general and charged with preparing the home guard

Brigadier General Simon Bolivar Buckner. An old friend and West Point underclassman of Grant's, Buckner commanded the Confederate right wing at Fort Donelson. He was left to surrender the Fort after Floyd and Pillow escaped. *Courtesy of the Library of Congress.*

to defend the state. Within six months, Buckner's troops had become better organized, drilled and armed than most Regular Army units in the area—Union or Confederate. Unfortunately, the home guard was also seen as more in sympathy with the Confederates, and its growing strength alarmed some in the state government. In July, the guard was ordered to stack its arms, which led Buckner to resign. Having not openly declared for the Confederacy yet, he was twice offered a brigadier general's commission in the U.S. Army but declined. By September, he had moved into Tennessee and was waiting when Johnston's train pulled in. Three days later, Simon B. Buckner was a brigadier general in the Confederate army, commanding four thousand men whom he loaded onto train cars in Nashville. The following day, Buckner and his men occupied Bowling Green.[20]

Buckner's job was not just to occupy Bowling Green, ninety miles from Louisville, but to push his area of influence as far north as he could and make his force seem more dangerous than it really was. Johnston wanted to give the impression that he was stronger than was the case and that he was planning an offensive move against Louisville or even Cincinnati in the near future. This, he hoped, would keep the Federals from planning their own move south and buy him some time. Accordingly, Buckner's men began to aggressively patrol north from Bowling Green as far as the Green River near Munfordville, Buckner's hometown.

By early October, General Anderson had asked to be relieved for health reasons, and Sherman, quite reluctantly, accepted command of the department. Already pessimistic about the situation, he wrote to a friend about his new promotion: "I am forced into the command of this department against my will, and it would take 300,000 troops to fill half the calls for troops."[21]

By now, Johnston's plan was working. Sherman believed that he was confronted with overwhelming Confederate forces. Even the common soldier in the Confederate army was fooled by the propaganda. The following is an excerpt from a letter, written home to Tennessee from Bowling Green, by a Confederate cavalryman one day after Johnston moved his headquarters there from Nashville:

> *Bowling Green*
> *Oct 14 1861*
>
> *Dear Anna*
> *...I am sorry you have been so distressed by the false stories with regard to my being captured by the enemy. It is true I have been in some perilous places in passing through an enemy county where they were lying in ambush on all sides. I helped take several of them prisoners but they did not disturb me. I was taken sick and did not go the whole scout. Our battalion are all gone to green river or some where in that section...There are 50 or 60 thousand troops here now. They are going on still north of this. There is a great battle expected in a short time up about Louisville...Burton Warfield Co "D" 2nd Batt. TN Cav.*[22]

When this letter was written, Johnston had just brought General William J. Hardee and his men over the river from Arkansas, bringing his troop strength at Bowling Green up to about twelve thousand men. If a soldier in Johnston's army could be mistaken about the strength of his own forces by a factor of five, imagine what rumors were making their way to Sherman's headquarters.

By early November, the Federal command structure was set to change once more. George McClellan replaced Winfield Scott as the commanding general of the army and immediately changed both commanders in the West. Major General Henry Halleck was sent to St. Louis to replace John C. Fremont, and Brigadier General Don Carlos Buell was sent to Louisville to replace Sherman, who had already asked to be relieved. McClellan gladly accommodated him. Sherman's increasingly frantic dispatches about

Major General Henry Wager Halleck. He assumed command of the Federal Western Department, with headquarters in St. Louis in November 1861. Overall commander of the Fort Henry and Fort Donelson campaign, Halleck did not like Grant and tried repeatedly to find a way to get him replaced. *Courtesy of the Library of Congress.*

the huge Confederate army that he thought he was facing had convinced McClellan that the Ohioan was becoming unbalanced. Sherman was sent to St. Louis, where General Halleck reported that he seemed demoralized and "stampeded." McClellan had a simpler explanation: "Sherman's gone in the head." Halleck gave Sherman a leave of absence, and his wife, Ellen, took him home to Ohio.[23]

Finally, the stage was set, and the senior commanders were in place for the coming campaign. As is often the case, however, it would be the men further down the chain of command—at the operational level—who would determine the outcome, and here the Union had the advantage.

Chapter 7

First Blood

The two months since the end of Kentucky neutrality had seen a steady increase in Ulysses S. Grant's command based at Cairo, Illinois. By November 1, he was commanding almost twenty thousand troops and had a group of subordinate commanders he was trying to build into a team. As with any team, it was something of a mixed bag. When Grant had mustered his first command, the Twenty-first Illinois, into the Union army back in late June, two politicians had come to speak, and now both of them were working for him.

John Alexander McClernand was a Democratic politician and supporter of Stephen A. Douglas who became an equally strong supporter of Lincoln once the war began. Perhaps his greatest contribution in the days just after Fort Sumter was his efforts to hold the volatile and Confederate-sympathizing southern Illinois area for the Union. As a reward, he was made a brigadier general and was commanding a brigade at Cairo when Grant arrived to take command in early September. McClernand had high political ambitions and a disdain for what he called the "trade unionism" of West Pointers and Regular Army officers. He was described by one observer as having "a thirst for military renown and an extra high opinion of himself." The dealings between Grant and McClernand were correct, but there was the underlying feeling that McClernand also had his own agenda. Grant knew that he needed watching.[24]

Serving under McClernand as a regimental commander was the other politician who had spoken at the swearing in of Grant's first regiment. John A. Logan was another Douglas Democrat who represented a district

Colonel John A. Logan, Thirty-first Illinois, with his wife, Mary, and children. Logan was seriously wounded on February 15. His wife, Mary, used her influence with the governor of Illinois to come to Fort Donelson and care for him. *Courtesy of the Library of Congress.*

in southern Illinois. At first, Logan's loyalties were suspect—his brother-in-law had actually gone south and joined the Confederate army—but he ultimately stayed loyal to the Union. Logan raised a regiment from among his constituents in a district riddled with Confederate sympathizers and was elected its leader. Now a colonel, he commanded the Thirty-first Illinois Infantry, proudly known by its men as the "Dirty First." It is said that "Black Jack" Logan fought, swore, drank, raced horses and played the violin with equal enthusiasm—and his men loved him.[25]

By the first of November, McClernand and Logan and their men had begun to grumble about their lot. They had been in the army several months and were getting tired of drilling and marching yet never seeing any real action. They were also tired of living in tents on the low and muddy land near Cairo—known as "Egypt" for good reason—where disease, rather than bullets, had carried off many of the Illinois farm boys. In a few days, however, their outgoing department commander, General Fremont, would accommodate them. Fremont was involved in an operation and needed a diversion from Grant and another brigadier general who commanded at Paducah with whom Grant would cooperate. If Grant's relationship with

Brigadier General John A. McClernand. U.S. representative from Illinois. McClernand owed his commission to political connections. Senior division commander under Grant, his units were mauled during the Confederate breakout attempt on February 15. *Courtesy of the Library of Congress.*

Brigadier General Charles Ferguson Smith. A career professional soldier and one of Grant's instructors at West Point, Smith commanded a division under Grant and personally led his men in an attack that secured much of the high ground on the Confederate right on February 15. *Courtesy of the Library of Congress.*

John McClernand was professional but watchful, his relationship with C.F. Smith was more complex and potentially more awkward.

While U.S. Grant seldom looked the part of a professional soldier and leader of men, Charles Ferguson Smith certainly did. Born in Philadelphia to an army family, Smith had graduated from West Point in the class of 1825, at age eighteen, and for the last thirty-six years he had been a soldier. By 1829, he was back at West Point as an instructor, and in 1838, a year before Grant arrived as a plebe, he became the commandant of cadets. For the years Ulysses S. Grant spent at the academy, the example for all the cadets of what an army officer should be was embodied in the person of First Lieutenant Charles F. Smith. Now, eighteen years later at age fifty-four, newly promoted brigadier general C.F. Smith had come to command the troops at Paducah, Kentucky, and would shortly be incorporated into the department commanded by his former pupil, whose commission in this new army was senior to Smith's by three months. Of Grant's four subordinate general officers (or naval equivalent), three were at least ten years older, and two of them (Foote and Smith) were vastly more experienced, having between them seventy-five years of military service.[26]

In early September, Grant had taken Paducah on his own initiative, receiving permission from General Fremont after the fact, but during the next two months nothing more than local skirmishing broke the boredom. If McClernand and Logan and their men were getting restive, so was General Grant. Finally, on November 1, orders came from General Fremont to mount a series of demonstrations against the Confederates at Columbus, Kentucky. Fremont was pursuing Confederate troops under General Sterling Price in southeast Missouri and wanted General Polk at Columbus to be occupied on the Kentucky side of the river so that he would not consider sending reinforcements across the Mississippi to threaten Fremont's rear. This was to be Grant's job.

Here, at least, was something for the troops to do. Within the next few days, Grant had several units moving on both sides of the river, with four separate formations of troops operating on the Missouri side of the river. As for Columbus itself, General Smith was ordered to send two columns west from Paducah to threaten Columbus from the land side, while Grant would take about three thousand men downriver with two gunboats to confront them from the river. They should keep the Confederates at Columbus occupied, but none of these formations was expected to bring on a serious action. General McClernand at Cairo was notified on the evening of November 5 to have his three regiments ready to leave the next day, and two more regiments across the river at Birds Point were alerted as well.

Wednesday, November 6 dawned bright and clear, and the troops at Cairo and Bird's Point got busy cooking rations, cleaning weapons, loading haversacks and doing all of the other things a regiment does to prepare for action. At the wharves at Cairo, six contract steamers were tied up and made ready to receive their passengers. By 3:00 p.m., General McClernand's three regiments and one company of cavalry were filing aboard the transports, and by sundown, they were on their way across the river to pick up two more regiments of infantry, another company of cavalry and a six-gun artillery battery. By 9:00 p.m., they were on their way downriver, led by two gunboats—the *Tyler*, commanded by Commander Henry Walke, and the *Lexington*, commanded by Commander Roger Stembel; by Grant's own count, the total was 3,114 men.

Planning to arrive near Belmont soon after sunup, the flotilla tied up on the Kentucky shore two hours later to pass the rest of the night. Grant later reported that while they were stopped, he received a message to the effect that a loyal Union man had reported that the Confederates were landing troops at Belmont with the intent of attacking the columns that Grant had operating in southeast Missouri and possibly reinforcing Confederate troops under Jeff Thompson or Sterling Price. The accuracy or even the existence of the message has since been questioned, but at the time, it suited Grant's needs perfectly.

No one was more frustrated with the lack of action than Grant himself, and the early morning message he received on the riverboat gave him the excuse he needed. Although his little expedition was supposed to be only a demonstration, he now felt that this new information required him to land his troops on the Missouri side and deal with this new threat at the landing at Belmont, just across the river from Columbus. Accordingly, he gave the following order:

> *November 7, 1861—2 o'clock a.m.*
> *The troops composing the present expedition from this place will move promptly at 6 o'clock this morning. The gunboats will take the advance, and be followed by the First Brigade, under command of Brigadier General John A. McClernand, composed of all the troops from Cairo and Fort Holt. The Second Brigade, comprising the remainder of the troops of the expedition, commanded by Colonel Henry Dougherty, will follow. The entire force will debark at the lowest point on the Missouri shore*

where a landing can be effected in security from the rebel batteries. The point of debarkation will be designated by Captain Walke, commanding naval forces.

By order of Brigadier General U.S. Grant:
JOHN A. RAWLINS,
Assistant Adjutant-General.

And so began Ulysses S. Grant's first Civil War battle.

Escorted by the *Tyler* and the *Lexington*, Grant's force pushed off from the Kentucky shore soon after daylight, crossed to the Missouri side and by 8:30 a.m. had landed about three miles above Belmont Landing (what the Confederates called "Camp Johnston") and had his troops ashore. They were within the range of some of the heavy guns at Columbus but around a bend in the river and out of sight. Even so, they had been observed by scouts on the Kentucky shore, and the alarm had been sounded immediately. Instead of the large contingent of troops that Grant had been told to expect, at 8:30 a.m. that morning Belmont was held by only one Confederate regiment, some cavalry and one battery of artillery. When he landed, Grant outnumbered the Confederates almost five to one, but by the time his troops were able to close with the enemy, General Gideon Pillow had brought over four more regiments from Columbus, putting the sides at more or less equal strength.

By 10:30 a.m., the Federal column was closing on the Confederate position, and their skirmishers were meeting resistance. Grant had wanted a fight, and now he had found one. For the next three hours, the boys from Iowa and Illinois who had been clamoring for some action found about all they could handle, but by about 1:30 p.m., the Confederate line had given way. The Southern survivors fled along the riverbank, and the victorious Federals began to celebrate by looting the Confederate camp. General McClernand gave in to his political instincts and gave a rousing speech as the boys broke open trunks and gathered up captured weapons, flags and anything else that caught their fancy. Even General Grant could not restrain them, so he ordered the camp set on fire. Grant knew that the thing was far from over, and shortly, fire from the heavy guns across the river at Columbus began to fall on them. This did more to restore order than anything, and soon the regiments were reformed and marching back toward the landing.

The trip back to the transports proved to be a nightmare. Confederate reinforcements had landed while the Yankees were celebrating and dogged their flanks and rear the whole way, inflicting more casualties. It was almost sundown before the Federal troops were back aboard, with the gunboats having to keep the Rebels back with cannon fire as the last units boarded. Grant was the last man aboard. Prior to Belmont, Grant had only commanded a handful of men in actual combat, and that had been back in Mexico. Now he had a real battle under his belt, even if he did stretch his original orders almost to the breaking point. The cost for this day's education had been just over 600 men killed, wounded or captured—almost 20 percent of his force. Confederate losses were slightly more—maybe 650.

In view of what Grant would experience in the coming years of the war, Belmont seems like just a skirmish, but it was where he and some of his men drew first blood. Mistakes were made, to be sure, but Grant seemed to be able to learn from them. War is a constant learning process, and Belmont was Grant's first serious lesson. Within three months, he would have the chance to put those lessons to good use in Tennessee.[27]

Chapter 8

Time Grows Short

The defenses on the Cumberland have so far been almost entirely overlooked.
—Colonel Adolph Heiman, October 18, 1861

The sites for the two forts on the Tennessee and the Cumberland Rivers had been selected and the work begun almost five months ago, but the above statement about the conditions at Fort Donelson was included in Colonel Adolph Heiman's report a month after General Johnston took overall command. Conditions at Fort Henry were a little better. The walls of the fort itself were in place, and nine artillery pieces were on site, but only four of them were sighted to fire down the river. Across the river, the high ground rose 170 feet above the river and, at a distance from the fort of only 1,500 yards, was well within the range of any decent field artillery battery the enemy might place there. No work had been done on that site at all. Above all, what worried the Confederates most was that the rains had begun and both rivers were rising. The comments of Gustavus A. Henry, for whom Fort Henry was named, summed up the situation in mid-October (Henry lived at Clarksville, just upstream from Fort Donelson, and would soon become one of Tennessee's senators in the Confederate Congress): "[T]here is nothing to prevent the enemy from harassing us on this [the Cumberland] and the Tennessee Rivers, both of which are now in fine boating order."[28]

Colonel Heiman's and Senator Henry's concerns seemed to be well founded, not only from the conditions of the two forts but also by the activities of the enemy. A few days earlier, the Union gunboat *Conestoga* had steamed up the Tennessee to within sight of Fort Henry and then, a day or so later,

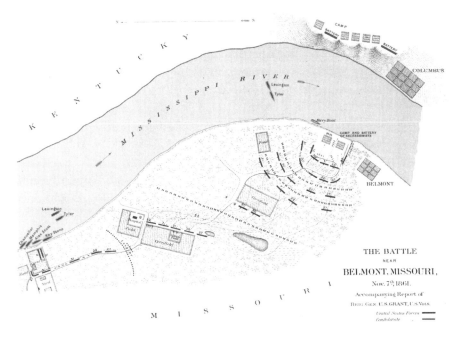

Contemporary map of the Battle of Belmont, November 7, 1861. *Courtesy of Wikimedia Commons.*

went up the Cumberland as far as Eddyville, about forty-five miles below Fort Donelson. With the rivers rising, it was becoming obvious that both Fort Henry and Fort Donelson were within the reach of Union gunboats, and therefore of their transports as well, which meant Union infantry.

The reports sent back from the first gunboat reconnaissance of the two rivers and of Fort Henry illustrated one of the primary problems that plagued both armies in the run up to the first major battle—lack of accurate intelligence. Lieutenant Ledyard Phelps, commander of the *Conestoga*, sent a report simply stating that Fort Henry, from two miles away, looked to be a formidable fortification, with heavy guns and room for a fairly large garrison. General Smith, at Paducah, then followed with his own report stating that his sources put the number of guns at twenty and the garrison at two thousand men.

Two days later, Colonel Heiman, commanding Fort Henry, reported to his commander his actual strength—330 men and nine guns, only four of which would cover the river. Fortunately for the Confederates, the Union forces had no good, firsthand observations of Fort Donelson yet, and so were unaware of its essentially defenseless condition. The lack of good intelligence was a problem common to both sides, with wildly inaccurate estimates mixed in with more realistic ones—and the commanders, both Blue and Gray, willing to believe the worst.[29]

As November came, the cast of characters began to change. By the middle of the month, both Federal commanders had been replaced. Brigadier General Don Carlos Buell had taken over in Louisville from a mentally frazzled William T. Sherman, and Major General Henry W. Halleck had assumed a command in serious disarray at St. Louis from John C. Fremont. Neither of these changes relieved Confederate commander Albert Sidney Johnston of his primary problems, however. He still had a nearly 450-mile line to defend east of the Mississippi with forces stretched impossibly thin. His men needed everything. He had a few troops armed with modern Enfield rifles that had come through the Northern blockade while others had only flintlock muskets that went back to the War of 1812—and still others had only shotguns they had brought from home or nothing at all. In exasperation with the constant call for arms, President Davis even suggested at one point

Brigadier General Don Carlos Buell. Assumed command of the Federal Department of the Ohio, with headquarters in Louisville in November 1861. Buell was Henry W. Halleck's rival for command of a unified department. *Courtesy of the Library of Congress.*

that pikes might be used. On top of everything else, it seemed that every one of Johnston's commanders in the field, from the Cumberland Gap to the Mississippi River, was certain that he was in imminent danger of attack and needed all available help immediately sent to his rescue.

For Johnston, getting the forts on the two rivers in some state of readiness was proving to be a nagging problem. Colonel Heiman and Lieutenant Colonel McGavock had done what they could, but manpower and matériel were scarce. Several professional engineers had come and gone and filed reports, but not much progress had been made, especially at Fort Donelson. Johnston needed someone to take over both projects and get them done, and by the middle of November, he thought he had found him.

Lloyd Tilghman was born in Maryland, but by 1852, he and his family were living in Paducah, Kentucky, and by 1858, he had become the chief engineer for the Mobile & Ohio Railroad. Tilghman was one of that large group of West Point graduates that had left the army for civilian pursuits. Tilghman, however, like many others, went back in the army during the Mexican-American War and so was a combat veteran. Tilghman had also been active in the Kentucky State Guard before the war and then commanded its western division during the summer of Kentucky neutrality. When the guard was disbanded, Tilghman followed his old commander, Simon B. Buckner, into Confederate service and by November 1861 was a brigadier general commanding the area around Hopkinsville, Kentucky. On November 17, Tilghman received this order:

> *HEADQUARTERS WESTERN DEPARTMENT, Bowling Green, Ky., November 17, 1861.*
> *Brigadier General LLOYD TILGHMAN, Hopkinsville, Ky.:*
>
> *In turning over your command at Hopkinsville, in pursuance of Special Orders, Numbers 89, you will repair to the Cumberland, and assume command of Forts Donelson and Henry and their defenses and the defenses of the intermediate country. You will push forward the completion of the works and their armament with the utmost activity, and to this end will apply to the citizens of the surrounding country for assistance in labor, for which you will give them certificates for amounts due for such labor. You will make your requisitions for quartermaster, subsistence, and ordnance stores upon the chiefs of the several departments at these headquarters…I will ask Governor Harris to-morrow for four additional armed companies, which he will send to Fort Donelson. These, with the six companies now there, will make up a regiment, when organized by*

Brigadier General Lloyd Tilghman. Commander of Fort Henry, Tilghman stayed behind with a company of artillerymen to defend the fort, allowing the rest of the garrison to escape to Fort Donelson. *Courtesy of the Library of Congress.*

the election of field officers. The colonel will command the fort. You will then
order Lieutenant-Colonel MacGavock to return to his regiment at Fort Henry…

By command of General Johnston:
W.W. MACKALL,
Assistant Adjutant-General. [30]

General Tilghman assumed his new command and did a complete tour of the two forts. By early December, he was ready with his first impressions. Tilghman, like everyone else, was not happy with the unfortunate location of Fort Henry, vulnerable as it was to both the river and the heights across the way. At one point, he said, "The history of military engineering records no parallel to this case." To General Polk, his direct superior, he reported on December 2: "[I]t is but too plain that instant and powerful steps must be taken to strengthen not only the two forts in the way of work, but the armament must be increased materially in number of pieces of artillery as well as in weight of metal." [31]

As with most other places in the Confederate command, Fort Donelson and Fort Henry suffered from muddled and conflicting lines of authority. Tilghman was ordered to the rivers by General Johnston but worked directly for General Polk in Columbus while also dealing directly with General Johnston in Bowling Green. He even sent a personal appeal directly to President Davis. Tilghman supposedly commanded Fort Donelson but clashed with Chief Engineer Gilmer, who worked directly for General Johnston and gave his own orders for obstructing the river near the water batteries—orders that Tilghman countermanded. In addition, the military command structure had to work with the civilian government in Tennessee, as well as in Alabama and Mississippi and the other Confederate states, because in many cases they were the ones raising and arming the militia units that were being fed into the Confederate army. Command and control problems and confused lines of responsibility would continue to plague the Confederates and eventually be a major contributor to the disaster to come.

Finally, early in December, Tilghman got some good news. En route down the Tennessee River was the Twenty-seventh Alabama regiment along with five hundred slave laborers, scheduled to begin work on the high ground across the river that would protect Fort Henry from that direction. It would be named Fort Heiman, for the Prussian construction superintendent and commander of the Tenth Tennessee. Slowly, progress began to be made, and Tilghman's forces and armament began to increase at both forts.

Christmas at Fort Henry turned out to be quite a festive affair. To Colonel Heiman's considerable dismay, Kentucky moonshine was provided by a local vendor, and a wagon load of food and gifts arrived from Fort Donelson, all courtesy of Lieutenant Colonel Randal McGavock. His Irishmen of the Tenth Tennessee hosted all comers, and Christmas Mass was said by Father Vincent Browne, the Tenth's regimental chaplain; the Mass was also said to have been attended by a surprising number of Alabama Baptists. Later, carols were sung by an ad hoc choir that is remembered as being "a wee bit lacking in harmony, but outstanding in volume." For a little while, the men were comfortable and life was good, but it would not last.[32]

While General Tilghman was trying to bring some order and progress to the two river forts, a new officer was operating in the area, but unlike Tilghman, he had no formal military education. What he knew of fighting he had learned the hard way, in the small towns and the backwoods of Mississippi and Tennessee. At age sixteen, Nathan Bedford Forrest had taken on the support of his entire family upon the death of his father and, by the summer of 1861, had become a rich and influential man in southwest Tennessee and northwest Mississippi. He was a former Memphis city alderman, and his plantations in Mississippi produced one thousand bales of cotton that year, which would have been worth more than $50,000 at the time. He also ran a business that bought and sold slaves. In June 1861, one month short of his fortieth birthday, Forrest joined a cavalry company forming in Memphis as an ordinary trooper.

A month later, the troops in west Tennessee were mustered into the Confederate army, and both Governor Harris and General Polk agreed that a man of Forrest's means and influence—and talent—was wasted as a private soldier. Forrest was ask to form a new cavalry regiment, which he did, and was naturally elected its leader. By mid-October, Lieutenant Colonel Forrest had 650 men formed into eight companies, and near the end of the month, they all arrived at Fort Donelson.

Within a few days, though, Forrest had moved most of his men across the Cumberland and was operating in the vicinity of Hopkinsville, even ambushing the Union gunboat *Conestoga* while it was tied up at the landing at Canton, Kentucky, during one of its forays up the Cumberland. Christmas came and went, however, without the kind of action that a cavalry commander hopes for; three days later, though, he finally got his chance.

On December 28, while patrolling from Greenville toward Rumsey, Kentucky, with about 300 troopers, Forrest was advised by a local Confederate sympathizer—a beautiful young lady on horseback—that a Union cavalry force was just ahead. This turned out to be a patrol of 168 men under Major Murray, stationed at Calhoun, about ten miles away. Forrest urged his column on, and when they came in sight of the enemy, he started the fight himself, firing the first shot with a Maynard rifle. What followed was the kind of maneuvering, running fight for which Forrest would become famous. It also established Forrest's reputation as a leader who fought up front, in the thick of the action. During the pursuit of the Yankees as they fled toward the village of Sacramento, Forrest

Isham G. Harris, governor of Tennessee at the beginning of the Civil War and advocate of secession. *Courtesy of the Library of Congress.*

personally dispatched two men—one with a pistol and one with his saber—and took another captive. His men also saw, for the first time, the Forrest that so many Union commanders would come to fear.

In combat, all rational men are afraid. The men who survive learn to deal with the fear and continue to function. Many are brave, some even heroic, but Forrest seemed to be absolutely transformed. Forrest's second in command, Major D.C. Kelly a former Methodist minister, was amazed at the change that came over his commander when the fight started: "It was the first time I had seen the Colonel in the face of the enemy…I could scarcely believe him to be the man I had known for several months. His face was flushed…and his eyes, usually mild in their expression, were blazing with the intense glare of a panther's, springing upon its prey."

Sacramento was a brief and quite modest fight by the standards of those that were to come, but Lieutenant Colonel Forrest and his men had met the enemy in some force and not only survived but prevailed. If Belmont was Ulysses S. Grant's baptism of fire, then Sacramento was Nathan Bedford Forrest's. Grant prepared himself to lead men in mortal combat with years of study and experience; Forrest was simply born for it.[33]

Chapter 9

Time Runs Out

New Year's Day 1862 came in amid a lot of frustration in the upper command levels of both the Federal and Confederate armies in the Kentucky/Tennessee area of operations. For Confederate general Johnston, the frustrations were mainly just a continuation of the issues that had plagued him since he arrived to take command back in September: too much territory to defend; not enough of anything; whole regiments filled with boys just off the farm, drilling with antiquated arms inherited from their grandfathers; panicky subordinates; convoluted lines of authority and responsibility—the list was almost endless. Adding to all of these worries was the pressure of trying to anticipate and counter the Federal attack on his thin line that he knew would come soon.

On the Federal side, the territory opposing General Johnston's defensive line was still divided into two districts, and each had a new commander who had taken over about six weeks earlier. Some of their problems were of the same nature as those of their Southern counterparts—logistics and the training and arming of new recruits—but others were inherent in the Federal army system itself. Both new commanders realized immediately that it would be more efficient if the two jurisdictions were combined, and both realized that if the departments were merged the new commander would probably be one of them. This set up a natural rivalry, with neither current commander anxious to cooperate in some operation that might work to the advantage of his rival and give him an edge in the internal army political battles.

In Louisville, General Don Carlos Buell was also under another kind of pressure—the kind that comes direct from the White House. President Lincoln was quite sensitive to political pressures coming from loyal Tennesseans, led by Senator Andrew Johnson, to bring some relief to the many Union sympathizers in east Tennessee who were being strongly suppressed by the Confederate government. For some time, Lincoln had been pressing the army to mount an offensive through the Cumberland Gap and on toward Knoxville for this purpose. Politics aside, Lincoln was shrewd enough to realize that such a push would also put Federal troops astride the East Tennessee & Virginia Railroad, which was Virginia's direct connection with the Southern heartland west of the Alleghenies. For these reasons, General Buell had been under pressure to push troops in that direction since his first day on the job. Buell argued for a more indirect route—down the Louisville & Nashville Railroad through Bowling Green and into the Tennessee capital—but finally agreed to send General George Thomas with about five thousand men to confront the Confederate forces guarding the gap through the mountains, said to be on the Cumberland River near Mills Springs in southeast Kentucky. Thomas and his men set off on New Year's Day.

At his headquarters in St. Louis, Major General Henry Wager Halleck's frustrations were also of a different sort. Halleck had arrived in late November to take over a department that was on the brink of administrative chaos. He also inherited a large ironclad gunboat project and a subordinate brigadier general who had just, seemingly on the spur of the moment, brought on an engagement that resulted in six hundred casualties. Ulysses S. Grant had not made a good first impression. If he was anything, Henry Halleck was tidy, and to him, Grant's slightly scruffy appearance and the seemingly impromptu fight at Belmont did not inspire confidence. Far from considering Grant an asset, by the end of January Halleck was actively seeking to replace him.

Henry Halleck's nickname in the Old Army was "Old Brains," and for good reason. Halleck and Grant missed each other at West Point by a few months—Halleck graduated third in the class of 1839, and Grant showed up a few weeks later as an incoming plebe. During the next twenty years, Halleck became known as an academic, a consummate administrator and, not surprisingly, as a master of army internal politics. As far as strategy and tactics were concerned, he was not only a supremely "by the book" soldier, he actually wrote the book. His 1846 work *Elements of Military Art and Science* was required reading for many of the men who would command in the current conflict.[34] One of Grant's biographers, Geoffrey Perret, summed up Henry Halleck this way: "A man of much learning, and not a day of combat experience…Halleck was fussy, idiosyncratic—a fountain that spurted theories of war, but a dry creek in action. He could no more be bold than Grant could be patient."[35]

On the instructions of General McClellan, Halleck ordered on January 6 that a reconnaissance be made in support of General Buell's move into southeast Kentucky, which involved Grant leading a column south from Cairo toward Mayfield, Kentucky, and General C.F. Smith moving south from Paducah toward Murray. General McClernand, with Grant along, conducted the western portion, just to the east of the Confederate position at Columbus. They slogged along muddy roads in miserable weather for eleven days, crossing the river back to Cairo on January 20. General Smith, moving farther east, along the Tennessee River, had a more productive patrol. Two days after Grant's expedition returned to Cairo, Smith asked Lieutenant James Shirk, now commanding the gunboat *Lexington*, which was supporting Smith's advance, to take him and two of his staff up the river for a direct look at Fort Henry. Shirk was happy to oblige, having made several trips to the fort already. The *Lexington* approached within two miles of the fort, threw a few shells into it, received one in return that fell short and then retired down the river. Smith now had seen the fort for himself and was convinced that it could be taken. Back in Cairo, Grant had already come to the same conclusion.[36]

As soon as Grant got back across the Ohio to his headquarters, he fired off a telegram to Halleck in St. Louis, asking permission to come and speak to his commander about a pressing issue. Permission was granted, reluctantly, Grant would later say, but by January 23 he was waiting in Halleck's office, map case in hand, to press his case for an immediate move up the Tennessee to capture Fort Henry, but Grant's timing was unfortunate. Halleck was just recovering from a bout of measles and was in no mood to be lectured to on strategy by his subordinates. Grant had barely gotten his maps unfolded before he was advised that strategy and tactics was the domain of the major general commanding the department, and when he needed Brigadier General Grant's advice, he would let him know. End of meeting. Grant, in his own memoirs, stated that Halleck acted as if his proposal was "preposterous" and that he returned to Cairo "very much crestfallen."

General Halleck had, in fact, already decided to move on Fort Henry—it was the obvious axis of advance into Tennessee—he just wasn't ready yet, and he certainly didn't want Grant leading it. Halleck was trying to get Grant replaced. He had in mind retired general Ethan Allen Hitchcock, but the sixty-three-year-old declined the offer. Halleck, at the same time, was also pressing his political campaign with General McClellan to be made commander of a united Western Department, with Buell under him. Historian and Grant scholar Jack Hurst probably captured the essence of

Approximate location of Fort Henry as seen today from the site of Fort Heiman, across the Tennessee River. *Author's Collection.*

Halleck's reaction to Grant's visit: "Halleck did not dismiss Grant from their uncordial interview because he found the idea of an attack on Fort Henry preposterous, as Grant put it. What Halleck considered preposterous was that an underling, especially such an unimpressive one as Grant, should presume to advise Henry Halleck on anything."[37]

While the Federals were marching up and down over the countryside in the cold, wet weather, Lloyd Tilghman and his men were working feverishly at both Fort Henry and Fort Donelson, trying to be ready for the attack that they expected any day. Tilghman shuttled back and forth between the two forts, urging the work forward. Fort Henry now had several guns mounted and bearing on the river, including a ten-inch gun that would be impressive, even against ironclads. Tilghman's Alabama men were also working across the river on the site of long-neglected Fort Heiman, and Smith's close approach impressed on him again that one regiment with a decent battery of field guns on that hill could shut down Fort Henry entirely.

Elsewhere, the Confederates were strengthening the center of their line as best they could. Richmond had finally answered General Johnston's repeated request for troops by transferring Brigadier General John B. Floyd's small brigade (four Virginia regiments, maybe 1,200 men) to Bowling Green. At Columbus, Gideon Pillow had gotten into one of his frequent quarrels with General Polk and resigned in a huff just before Christmas but had since

Brigadier General Gideon J. Pillow, lawyer, politician and citizen-soldier. Second in command at Fort Donelson, he ordered his troops back into the Confederate lines after clearing the way for the escape of the army on February 15. Early the next morning, Pillow escaped across the river. *Courtesy of the Library of Congress.*

been brought back to command the supply depot at Clarksville. By the end of January, Johnston could muster, in the territory from the Tennessee River at Fort Henry east through Central Kentucky, about 30,000 men—about 5,000 between the two river forts, with the other 25,000 mostly around Bowling Green and spread out north along the Green River. Against this, Grant commanded about 20,000 at Cairo and Paducah, not counting recently promoted Flag Officer Foote's naval contingent, and General Buell had about 56,000 in central and east Kentucky.[38]

On Sunday morning, February 2, 1862, Father Browne, chaplain for the Tenth Tennessee, celebrated what turned out to be the last Mass the Irishmen would hear at Fort Henry—and then it began to rain.[39]

Chapter 10

"Make Your Preparations to Take and Hold Fort Henry"

U lysses S. Grant may have come back from St. Louis like a scolded schoolboy—"crestfallen" as he says—but he was still convinced that he was right. In this case, he also had two important allies. Both General Smith at Paducah, who had actually seen the place, and Flag Officer Foote of the navy agreed with Grant as to the need to attack Fort Henry at the earliest moment. Accordingly, five days after his unsuccessful meeting, Grant tried again, with this brief message to General Halleck:[40]

> CAIRO, *January 28,1862.*
> *Major General H. W. HALLECK,*
> *Saint Louis, Mo.*
>
> *With permission, I will take Fort Henry, on the Tennessee, and establish and hold a large camp there.*

The next day, Grant sent another, longer message, saying essentially the same thing. Grant had also been conferring with Flag Officer Foote, since any move up the Tennessee and Cumberland would have to involve large-scale naval support, and Foote also felt that the time was right. The ironclad gunboats were finally ready. The last couple of weeks had seen them commissioned, and except for recruiting more crew members, they were ready for their first test in combat. On the same day that Grant sent his first message, Foote sent one of his own. Possibly knowing that Grant was not in the best of favor at headquarters, Foote takes credit for the idea himself:

CAIRO, January 28, 1862.
Major-General HALLECK.

General Grant and myself are of the opinion that Fort Henry, on the Tennessee River, can be carried with four ironclad gunboats and troops, and be permanently occupied. Have we your authority to move for that purpose when ready?

A.H. FOOTE, Flag-Officer
• *NOTE.—I made the proposition to move on Fort Henry first to General Grant.*[41]

Unknown to both Grant and Foote, Halleck's own thinking had been changing since the St. Louis meeting. Two things had happened to influence him. The first had a direct bearing on Halleck's ongoing personal campaign to be made the commander of a new, consolidated Western Department, which would be a political victory over his perceived rival, General Buell in Louisville. Unfortunately—for Halleck, at least—one of Buell's men had just won a significant victory in eastern Kentucky. In January 1862, victories were scarce for the Federal army, so while it was good for the Union, Halleck saw it as a setback to his own agenda.

On New Year's Day, Buell had finally sent Brigadier General George Thomas in pursuit of the Confederate army blocking the way to east Tennessee. As mentioned earlier, this campaign had the personal interest of President Lincoln. On January 19, after slogging along atrocious roads for more than two weeks, the two forces met in the rain near Mill Springs, Kentucky, and the Confederates were eventually routed by Thomas's men. Some Confederates were seen breaking their antiquated flintlock muskets over tree stumps since they couldn't get their damp powder to prime the old guns. Confederate general Felix Zollicoffer was killed, and his army fell apart, leaving much of their equipment as they crossed to the south bank of the Cumberland River. If Thomas could have supplied his army in that desolate country, he might have almost walked into either Knoxville or Nashville. As it was, he eventually had to withdraw. The eastern part of General Albert S. Johnston's line was shattered, but the Federals couldn't follow up.

Even though it was not decisive, a victory like Mill Springs by one of General Buell's subordinates could very well give him the lead in the race

Brigadier General Felix K. Zollicoffer. He commanded Albert Sidney Johnston's troops in east Tennessee and eastern Kentucky. Zollicoffer was killed at Mills Springs, Kentucky, on January 19, 1862. *Courtesy of the Library of Congress.*

for department command. What Halleck needed was a victory of his own— preferably an even bigger one—and soon. Right now, however, the only one of Halleck's subordinates who was ready with a plan was Ulysses S. Grant. Halleck wasn't any more impressed with Grant now than he had been a week before, but Grant and Foote's plan was the only one that he could put in motion quickly.

The other factor in Halleck's decision was a piece of information—military intelligence that had come through army headquarters in Washington. For Halleck, this was the clincher. On January 30, Halleck sent Grant the following message:

SAINT LOUIS, January 30,1862.
Brigadier General U.S. GRANT, Cairo, Ill.

Make your preparations to take and hold Fort Henry. I will send you written instructions by mail.

H.W. Halleck, Major General

In those instructions, which are dated the same day, was this statement, which explained Halleck's change of heart: "A telegram from Washington says that Beauregard left Manassas four days ago with fifteen regiments for the line of Columbus and Bowling Green. It is therefore of the greatest importance that we cut that line before he arrives."[42]

Fifteen regiments could easily mean 7,500 fresh reinforcements under the hero of Fort Sumter and Bull Run. Added to the Union's already greatly inflated estimates of Johnston's strength, this was serious news indeed. Even if Grant had to lead the campaign, delay was no longer an option.

When Halleck's order came giving the permission to attack Fort Henry with all possible speed, Grant's headquarters at Cairo erupted with joy. John Rawlins pounded the walls with his fists, men threw their hats in the air and cheered and the normally taciturn Grant is said to have actually laughed out loud. At last, they were really going to war.[43]

Suddenly, there were a thousand things to do, but Grant, with his army, and Foote, with his gunboats and transports, had worked together often enough that things went quickly. Small detachments would be left behind to secure Bird Point on the Missouri shore and Cairo on the Illinois side, but the rest of General John McClernand's division would be loaded on transports and sent to Paducah and, from there, up the Tennessee. At Paducah, General C.F. Smith's division would form the rest of the expedition. Altogether, Grant would have at least fifteen thousand troops initially at Fort Henry, with constant reinforcements bringing his forces to over twenty-five thousand before the campaign at Fort Donelson was over.

Halleck's first message, as well as the longer, more detailed instructions, are both dated Thursday, January 30, but probably didn't arrive together. It may have been as late as Saturday, February 1, before the detailed instructions were in hand. By the next day, February 2, Grant's first division under McClernand was loading onto transports at Cairo, on its way upriver to Paducah. Grant's rush to get started was, ironically, due more to the knowledge that Halleck could change his mind and recall him at any time

John Rawlins. A captain at Fort Donelson and Grant's assistant adjutant general, Rawlins would stay with Grant through the war, eventually becoming a brevet major general. *Courtesy of the Library of Congress.*

than to concern about his opposition at Fort Henry. By 3:00 p.m. the next day (February 3), Grant, Foote and McClernand were all at Paducah, waiting for the transports with the First Division. When they arrived, they were taken on up the river to within a few miles of Fort Henry, landing at about 4:30 a.m. on Tuesday, February 4. Even with the number of steamers available due to the closing of the Mississippi below Cairo, Grant's entire army could not be carried at one time, but the past six months of drilling, skirmishing and working with the navy had paid off. Grant and Foote were in the process of inventing the science of combined army/navy operations that would become so familiar at places like Iwo Jima and Normandy, having moved almost seven thousand men more than a hundred miles and landing them safely almost within sight of Fort Henry.

McClernand had landed his men a cautious eight miles below Fort Henry, but when Grant arrived, he wanted them moved closer. The closer they could land to the fort, the less wilderness they would have to march through to get there when the time came. The limit to how close they could land would depend on the effective range of the fort's guns, so Grant, in his usual straightforward way, simply boarded the ironclad *Essex*, which had been escorting the transports, and asked Commander William Porter if he could draw some fire from the Confederates. Porter motored up and fired a few rounds into the fort, but nothing happened. Not having his question answered, Grant ordered the *Essex* to put about and return to the landing site, but just at this time, the fort finally replied. Of the eleven guns the fort had bearing down on the river by this time, seven did not have the range and two had no ammunition, which left only the ten-inch Columbiad and the twenty-four-pound rifle, which was chosen to engage the *Essex*. At two and a half miles, the rifle's first round cut down some trees on the bank near the gunboat, and the second round barely missed Grant and Porter, on the stern deck, tore through the captain's cabin, smashing his crockery, exited the other side of the boat and fell in the river. The Confederate gunners had scored a hit with their second round fired in the war—at over four thousand yards!

Grant had seen enough. He moved McClernand's men back just out of range and then boarded one of the transports returning to Paducah to pick up General C.F. Smith's Second Division. By 3:00 p.m., the First Division was ashore at the new landing and moving inland as it continued to rain— miserable for the men but good for the gunboats. The rising river had revealed one of the Confederates' more experimental attempts to defend Fort Henry. A group of new "torpedoes," set out in the channel, had been either ruined or torn loose by the current. These were a relatively new invention and were more like the later antiship mines that would be laid in coming wars, but they proved useless here. Between leakages spoiling the black power inside and the river at flood stage washing them away, they were no factor in the battle. Some were retrieved by the Union gunboats, but they caused no damage.[44]

When the Federals appeared, Colonel Heiman was in command at Fort Henry because General Tilghman had gone to Fort Donelson to inspect the work there. Confederate pickets had witnessed the arrival of the gunboats and transports and launched rockets to alert the fort. At sunrise on that Tuesday morning, Colonel Heiman sent a rider to Fort Donelson with the news and posted more scouts forward to keep an eye on the Federal troops. Fort Henry had just over 2,600 troops dedicated to it, but they were spread out. Two regiments were across the river at the site of Fort Heiman, and two more were up the river at Paris Landing. Heiman understood that these forces should be consolidated but waited for final orders from Tilghman. It is a measure of Fort

Henry's predicament that the unit both Tilghman and Heiman considered their best and most effective was Randal McGavock's Irishmen of the Tenth Tennessee, who were all armed with flintlocks from the War of 1812.

While the two forces began to get the measure of each other on February 4, Lloyd Tilghman at Fort Donelson, twelve miles away, was getting anxious. He had heard the cannon fire as the fort and the gunboats had their preliminary encounter and Grant found their range, and at 4:00 p.m., Colonel Heiman's courier arrived with the news of the landings below the fort. General Tilghman left Fort Donelson under the command of Colonel John W. Head of the Thirtieth Tennessee with orders to form a reserve force and move it out about halfway between the two forts, in case they were needed at Fort Henry. Tilghman then set off for Fort Henry with Major Gilmer, the chief engineer and an escort from the Ninth Tennessee Cavalry under Lieutenant Colonel George Gantt. This small cavalry battalion had been pulled out of an instructional camp in mid-January and sent to Fort Donelson and had, as yet, seen no action.

General Tilghman and his escort rode hard and reached Fort Henry by 11:30 p.m. on the fourth, where he was brought up to date by Colonel Heiman. Everyone spent a fitful night, and at first light on the fifth, General Tilghman ordered that the works across the river at Fort Heiman be evacuated, with the exception of two companies of Alabama cavalry and a force of about forty Kentucky men called Padgett's Spy Company, which were left to harass the Yankees on the west side of the river as best they could. Back across the river came the Fifteenth Arkansas and the Twenty-seventh Alabama, to be added to the forces at Fort Henry. The rest of the Fifth was taken up with more aggressive reconnoitering on both sides and a skirmish between the cavalry companies of Captain Henry Milner (Confederate) and Captain James J. Dollins (Union) that claimed one man on each side. Late in the afternoon, General C.F. Smith's division began arriving, with two brigades landing on the west side of the Tennessee and one brigade on the east. It was after 11:00 p.m. on the fifth before all of Grant's army was finally assembled, but General Tilghman at Fort Henry had a good idea what he was up against. Although Tilghman didn't have the exact numbers for the Federal army, he would not have been surprised to learn that he was outnumbered about five to one, not counting the gunboats. He was not exaggerating when he lamented later, in his official report, "the wretched military position of Fort Henry and the small force at my disposal."

However valid Lloyd Tilghman's complaints were, he would have to make do with what he had. Time had run out.

Chapter 11

Fire on the River

It had rained all night as General Smith's men were landing, and due to the lateness of their arrival, General Grant delayed the start of the attack on Fort Henry until late the next morning. Dawn on February 6 saw a lot of black smoke coming from the direction of Panther Island, indicating that the Federal gunboats were getting up steam, and everybody at Fort Henry knew that the fight would not be long in coming. General Tilghman and Major Gilmer, the chief engineer, had been to the western shore but had returned by about 10:00 a.m.. The artillerymen in the fort, and the army garrison guarding the approaches, then took their places, and everybody waited. It was obvious now that the attack would come from the river and the land simultaneously.

Fort Henry was now armed with sixteen cannon, eleven of which could bear on the river approaches:

- Seven thirty-two-pounders—short- to medium-range weapons. They were effective against wooden ships but of unknown effectiveness against the new ironclads. Their range was about a mile, so they would not be fired until the gunboats got within about 1,500 yards or less.
- Two forty-two-pounders—obsolescent army pieces for which no proper ammunition was available. The crews at Fort Henry probably tried firing them with improvised charges because one is said to have burst.
- One twenty-four-pound rifled cannon—the gun that had fired upon General Grant and the *Essex*. As it had demonstrated, it could

The Fort Henry campaign. *Courtesy of Hal Jespersen, www.posix.com/CW.*

be deadly out to at least three miles and was probably the most versatile and effective piece in the Confederate arsenal.

- One ten-inch Columbiad—the most powerful gun at Fort Henry. Normally a coastal defense gun, it weighed more than 15,000 pounds, and with a charge of 15 to 20 pounds of powder, it could fire a 128-pound solid shot more than five thousand yards with accuracy. It had a defective carriage, though, and the recoil was so ferocious that it was at risk of dismounting itself with every shot, but one solid hit could be fatal.[45]

General Grant had set 11:00 a.m. as the start time for the attack, with the gunboats closing on the river while the army advanced along both banks.

USS *Carondelet*, the City Class ironclad that fought at both Fort Henry and Fort Donelson. *Courtesy of the Naval Historical Center.*

USS *Conestoga*, a converted "timber clad" gunboat that fought at Fort Henry and Fort Donelson, as well as in the Tennessee River raid. *Courtesy of the Naval Historical Center.*

With the infantry having to ford swollen streams and march through a soggy wilderness, the new gunboats, even bucking the current, soon pulled ahead of the ground forces. Shortly before noon, the defenders of Fort Henry could see the Union gunboats maneuvering into position about three miles

USS *Lexington*, a converted "timber clad" gunboat that fought at Fort Henry and in the Tennessee River raid. *Courtesy of the Naval Historical Center.*

USS *Tyler*, a converted "timber clad" gunboat that fought at Fort Henry and Fort Donelson, as well as in the Tennessee River raid. *Courtesy of the Naval Historical Center.*

away. The First Division consisted of the four ironclads—*Essex, Carondelet, Cincinnati* and *St. Louis*—advancing in line abreast. Behind them, at some distance, came the three Second Division timber clads, the *Lexington, Conestoga* and *Tyler*. Flag Officer Foote commanded the first division, with his flag on the *Cincinnati*, while Lieutenant Ledyard Phelps commanded the second division from the *Conestoga*.

The three new City Class boats—*Carondelet, Cincinnati* and *St. Louis*—mounted thirteen guns overall, but the three guns forward were kept pointed toward the enemy as much as possible because the heaviest armor was also up front. The iron plating only covered the forward one-half to two-thirds of the structure, making the boats vulnerable to shots to the rear or plunging fire to the wooden decks. The *Essex* was a special case—a standard riverboat converted to a gunboat and then covered with some iron plating. Consequently, it had a higher profile that made it an easier target.

Most of his crews may have been going into combat for the first time, but Flag Officer Andrew Hull Foote was not. A veteran of many encounters on the water all around the globe, he steadily advanced his First Division on Fort Henry, and at 1,700 yards he opened fire.[46] Fort Henry replied with its twenty-four-pound rifle and the ten-inch Columbiad, and the battle was on. Once the firing started, it could be heard for miles, and General McClernand's men, closing on the fort from the east side, and General Smith's men, struggling toward Fort Heiman on the west bank, cheered knowing that the attack had begun.

Initially, the fort replied with its two long-range guns, but the gunboats continued to close the distance so that, before long, all of the fort's guns were firing. The gunboats continued to close until they were only six hundred yards away and pounded the fort continuously. General Tilghman had moved all of his troops out of range of the shot and shell except for about seventy-five artillerymen manning the guns, and they were giving it back to the gunboats as fast as they could, scoring hit after hit at the close-range targets.

After half an hour or so of constant firing, the gunners in the fort scored a devastating hit. A Confederate shell hit the *Essex* and penetrated into the center of the ship, bursting one of its boilers. Live steam immediately swept the forward part of the ship, scalding many men, including both civilian pilots and the ship's commander, William "Dirty Bill" Porter, who managed to escape death by throwing himself out of a porthole. Powerless, the *Essex* drifted out of the fight and back downriver, where it was finally taken under tow by another vessel.[47]

Unfortunately for the defenders of Fort Henry, soon after they silenced the *Essex*, a series of disasters hit them as well. Their most effective piece, the twenty-four-pound rifle, burst, killing or disabling the entire crew; one of the thirty-two-pounders was hit and disabled; one of the forty-two-pounders also burst, causing more casualties; and, finally, the massive ten-inch Columbiad was silenced by a broken priming wire sealing the vent. After serving the guns for almost an hour, the crews were also at the end of their strength. General Tilghman himself served one of the thirty-two-pounders still firing for a while, but it was obvious by now that the end was near. Only four thirty-two-pounders were still able to fire, and the fort itself was in danger of being flooded by the Tennessee River. Had General Grant waited a couple of days to attack, it's quite possible that the Confederates would have been forced to abandon the fort without a fight simply because of the rising water.

Not that he was a defeatist, but Lloyd Tilghman had already decided that he stood no chance of holding Fort Henry. Everything he saw told him so. Before the battle ever started, he had decided to try and save the bulk of the garrison by defending the fort with only the artillerymen to buy time for the rest to retreat to Fort Donelson, where they might be able to make a stand. Accordingly, at the height of the battle with the gunboats, he passed command of the rest of the men to Colonel Adolphus Heiman with orders to get them safely to the Cumberland. In Grant's operations order, part of General McClernand's division's responsibilities had been to block just such a breakout attempt, but they couldn't cover the distance to the fort until Colonel Heiman and the rest of the Fort Henry garrison were well on their way.

General Tilghman and his small band of artillerymen had done all they could. Choosing to remain at the fort until the last rather than go with the retreating column to Fort Donelson, Tilghman ordered the flag lowered at 1:55 p.m.; the Battle of Fort Henry was over. Having been under construction for eight months, it had held out against the Union ironclads for less than two

Engraving of the attack on Fort Henry, published in *Harper's Weekly*, March 1, 1862. *Author's Collection*.

Brigadier General Lewis Wallace. The junior brigadier in Grant's army, Wallace was given the job of organizing the arriving reinforcements at Fort Donelson into a new division under his command. On February 15, his second day as a division commander, Wallace and his men deployed without orders and stopped the Confederate attack on the Federal right. *Courtesy of the Library of Congress.*

hours. Acting for Flag Officer Foote, Commander Stemble, of the flagship *Cincinnati* and Lieutenant Phelps, of the *Conestoga*, took a boat to the fort, raised the American flag and took General Tilghman back to meet with Flag Officer Foote for the formal surrender.

Across the river, General Smith and his men had finally worked their way to the site of Fort Heiman, only to find it deserted. Confederates had been there recently enough, however, that General Lew Wallace, one of Smith's brigade commanders, found dinner cooking—a block of pork "done to a turn" and cornbread—which he and General Smith shared. Across the river, they could see the Stars and Stripes flying over Fort Henry.[48]

On the east bank of the river, General McClernand's men finally reached the road south of the fort and sent some cavalrymen in pursuit of the escaped Confederates. First to catch up with Colonel Heiman's rear guard was a small group of cavalry from Stewart's company, which was soon joined by a detachment from the Fourth Illinois Cavalry under Lieutenant Colonel McCullough. These Union troopers harassed the rear of the Confederate column until sundown but caused no major damage. They did, however, manage to completely spook three companies of the Ninth Tennessee Cavalry under Lieutenant Colonel George Gantt who were supposed to be providing security. At the approach of the Fourth Illinois, the green Tennessee boys broke and stampeded back through the column. They had come to the field straight from training camp, and this was not their finest hour. As a result, Arkansas and Alabama infantrymen had to turn and meet the attack. In the resulting skirmish, the Confederates lost two officers and thirty-six men captured. The Union troopers broke off the pursuit as darkness came, and Colonel Heiman's group of survivors finally dragged into Fort Donelson about 2:00 a.m. on February 7, not realizing that their ordeal had just begun.[49]

The battle for Fort Henry was over quickly. Except for the skirmishes the day before and the pursuit of the retreating Confederate column, it had been a navy show, and Andrew Foote and his gunboats could rightly claim the honors. The new City Class boats had performed well, as had the rest of the fleet. In his report to the secretary of the navy, Foote summed up the new boat's performance:

> *The armored gunboats resisted effectually the shot of the enemy when striking the casemate. The Cincinnati, flagship, received 31 shot; the Essex, 15; the St. Louis, 7; and Carondelet, 6; killing 1 and wounding 9 in the Cincinnati and killing 1 in the Essex, while the casualties in the latter from steam amounted to 28 in number. The Carondelet and St. Louis met with no casualties.*[50]

Fort Henry had been the subject of much preparation at the operational level and much anxiety at the senior command levels of both armies for several months, and now it had fallen in less than two hours. General Grant had his first victory, even if the honors really belonged to the navy, and in his own mind at least, he was just getting started. On the day that Fort Henry fell, Grant sent the following message:

Headquarters District of Cairo, Fort Henry, February 6, 1862.

Fort Henry is ours. The gunboats silenced the batteries before the investment was completed. I think the garrison must have commenced the retreat last night. Our cavalry followed, finding two guns abandoned in the retreat. I shall take and destroy Fort Donelson on the 8th and return to Fort Henry.

U.S. Grant,
Brigadier-General.
Major General H.W. Halleck, Saint Louis, Mo.[51]

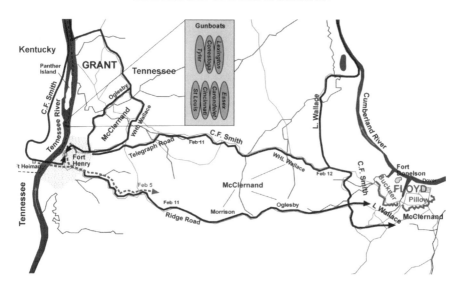

Fort Henry to Fort Donelson. *Courtesy of Hal Jespersen, www.posix.com/CW.*

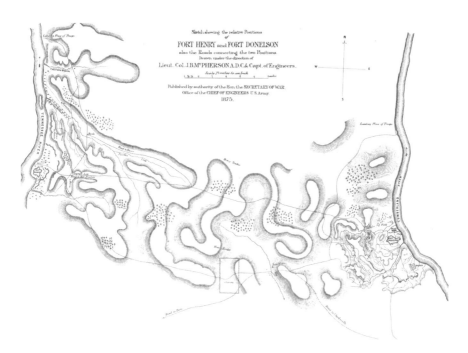

Contemporary map of Fort Henry and Fort Donelson, drawn by Lieutenant Colonel James B. McPherson, one of General Grant's aides. *Courtesy of the Library of Congress.*

Had Grant been able to do as he said—march to Fort Donelson on the eighth—he would have found a garrison of no more than seven thousand troops who were not remotely prepared to resist a determined attack by an army twice their number. As with several other things in his first campaign, however, Grant was much too optimistic about what could be accomplished in this rain-soaked wilderness. His advance to Fort Donelson would not begin on February 8, as he had told General Halleck. Instead of marching on to Fort Donelson in two days, it would take Grant's army six days to cover the twelve miles or so, which would make a great difference in what he would find when he arrived.

Chapter 12

Gunboats in the Heart of Dixie

From Fort Donelson, Colonel Heiman was able to send reports up the Cumberland to his superiors, and by the next day, word of the fall of Fort Henry was making its way through the Confederate chain of command. Unlike the Union victory in southeast Kentucky two weeks earlier, this one would not die in the wilderness for want of supplies. The loss of Fort Henry, and with it the control of the Tennessee River, was the strategic disaster that many in the South had seen coming for several months. Now that it was all but too late, help would be offered from the government in Richmond and other military commands, but the damage had been done. With Fort Henry gone, little hope was held out for Fort Donelson. While General Johnston and his staff were trying to decide what to do about the defense of the Cumberland and, ultimately, of Nashville itself, the Union navy was providing a practical demonstration of what its new control of the Tennessee River meant to the Confederacy.

Naval lieutenant Seth Ledyard Phelps, commanding the USS *Conestoga*, probably knew more about running gunboats on the Tennessee and Cumberland Rivers than any other man under Flag Officer Foote's command. Beginning back in October 1861, he had been making regular scouting trips up both rivers, as the water level would permit, and was the source for much of the firsthand intelligence that the Union had on the rivers and their forts. During the attack on Fort Henry, Phelps had commanded the three wooden boats as they fired at long distance while the ironclads did the closer work. Now that Fort Henry had fallen, Phelps had a mission of his own, which he began immediately. In his pocket, he probably had a copy of the special order that Flag Officer Foote had issued to him four days earlier back in Paducah:

SPECIAL ORDERS, ~ U.S. GUNBOAT TYLER,
No. 3. Paducah, February 2, 1862.

Lieutenant-Commanding Phelps will, as soon as the fort shall have surrendered and upon signal from the flagship, proceed with the Conestoga, Tyler, and Lexington up the river to where the railroad bridge crosses, and, if the army shall not already have got possession, he will destroy so much of the track as will entirely prevent its use by the rebels. He will then proceed as far up the river as the stage of water will admit and capture the enemy's gunboats and other vessels which might prove available to the enemy.

A.H. FOOTE,
Flag-Officer, Comdg. Naval Forces, Western Waters [52]

Taking the three wooden gunboats, Lieutenant Phelps was indeed about to raid as far up the Tennessee as he could.

Not long after Fort Henry surrendered, Lieutenant Phelps got his signal from the flagship *Cincinnati* and started upriver with his three timber clads. As stated in his orders, his first objective was the Memphis & Charleston Railroad bridge over the river, about twenty-five miles away. It was over this track that the Confederates could move forces and matériel between their large base at Columbus and General Johnston's army around Bowling Green, so it was high on General Halleck's list of targets. Phelps and his three gunboats arrived at the railroad bridge after dark on the sixth to find it recently abandoned and several steamers heading upriver a mile or so away. The huge 1,200-foot span had a section in the middle that swung to allow boats to pass, but the Confederates had closed it and jammed the machinery. A shore party got the bridge open in about an hour, and the *Conestoga* and the *Lexington* left in pursuit of the Rebel steamers. The slowest of the three boats, the *Tyler*, was left to tear up the track on both approaches—General Halleck had ordered that the bridge be left intact—and then follow at its best speed.

Where Foote's new City Class ironclads had the advantage in firepower and armor, the wooden boats had a significant advantage in speed, so it

City Class ironclad gunboats in the Ohio River off Cairo, Illinois. *Courtesy of the Naval Historical Center.*

only took about five hours for Phelps to overtake the fleeing transports. When the *Conestoga* pulled into sight, the Rebel captains began to set fire to three of the boats containing military stores, mainly munitions. When one exploded, Phelps pulled up short just in time. The other two boats contained ammunition, and even at one thousand yards, the explosion broke windows and caused other damage to the gunboat, as well as flattening a nearby house and covering the river for half a mile with falling bullets and debris. Phelps's command was now strung out on the river, so he stopped to let the others catch up before continuing.

After steaming all day on the seventh, Phelps found the steamer *Eastport* at Cerro Gordo in Hardin County, where the Confederates were in the process of converting it into an ironclad gunboat. Again, the *Tyler*, under Lieutenant Gwin, was left to guard the prize, while Phelps, with the *Conestoga* and the *Lexington*, continued up the river. By midday on the eighth—only forty-eight hours after the fall of Fort Henry—two Union gunboats sat at the landing at Florence, Alabama, over 150 steaming miles from the site of the battle. To say that their arrival was something of a shock would be an understatement. Lieutenant Phelps assured the anxious local leaders that their wives and daughters were safe, saying that he and his men "were neither ruffians nor savages" and agreeing to their request not to burn their railroad bridge. He then loaded all the military matériel he could find and started back down the river. Now aided by the current, he made better time and was back with the *Tyler* later that night. After capturing more weapons and learning that the very presence of the gunboats had frightened off a new Rebel regiment training nearby, Phelps and his command took the *Eastport* and two other vessels under tow and headed back downriver. By February 12, they were in Paducah, where Phelps made his report. The thing that Phelps found most interesting, so he says, was the amount of Union sentiment he found all along the river, even as far as Florence.[53]

While Lieutenant Phelps and his command were busy "showing the flag" up the Tennessee River, back at headquarters—both in St. Louis and in Bowling Green—the senior commanders were struggling to adapt to what had happened. In St. Louis, Henry Halleck was more than two hundred miles removed from the battlefield, but ever the micromanager, he was still sending a stream of orders down to Grant, many of which had little or no relation to the real situation on the ground. Grant's victory had done little to change Halleck's opinion of him, and he was still looking for any way to replace him. If anything, Grant's newfound success had begun to advance him—in Halleck's eyes, at least—from simply an undesirable subordinate to a possible rival for the rewards that Halleck felt were rightly his. Grant, with his hands full trying to manage a large army in the field, had no idea of Halleck's maneuvers behind the scenes, which was probably just as well. To Halleck's credit, however, he did continue to send Grant all of the supplies and reinforcements available. He did, after all, have a vested interest in the outcome. Halleck even managed to get his rival, General Buell, to contribute some regiments to the effort as well, even though they would arrive too late to help at Fort Donelson.

At Bowling Green, General Johnston had some critical decisions to make. Fortunately, he did not have to make them alone. Part of General Halleck's information from Washington had proved to be true. The famous General Pierre Gustave Toutant Beauregard was coming to reinforce Johnston's army—in fact, he was already there. Ordered west by President Davis mainly, it seems, as a gesture of support to his old friend Albert Sidney Johnston, Beauregard left Richmond on February 2 and, after a stop in Nashville, arrived at Bowling Green on the evening of the fourth, just as Grant's First Division was going into camp its first night at Fort Henry. Unfortunately for General Johnston, Beauregard was not bringing a single soldier with him, much less the fifteen regiments that Henry Halleck had feared.

Beauregard was not a well man, having just undergone surgery on his throat, but he and General Johnston met that same night so that the newly arrived general could be briefed on the present situation. Johnston laid out his forces east of the Mississippi, which came to roughly forty-eight thousand men, to face a Union force that, between Grant and Buell, still at Louisville,

General Pierre Gustave Toutant Beauregard. He arrived at Bowling Green two days before the fall of Fort Henry and took command of the part of the department west of the Tennessee River. On April 6, he took command of the army when Albert Sidney Johnston was killed. *Courtesy of the Library of Congress.*

numbered almost eighty thousand. Beauregard had been led to believe, from his briefings in Richmond, that Johnston's own army numbered almost seventy thousand, so the real situation came as something of a shock. The next day, he and Johnston inspected the works around Bowling Green, which in Beauregard's mind were bad enough, but Johnston's entire defensive line shouted trouble to Beauregard's orderly engineering mind. He quite correctly saw the river forts as the weak points and suggested that Bowling Green be abandoned and those forces—about twenty-five thousand men—be used to defend Forts Henry and Donelson. Johnston refused to give up Bowling Green and leave the way wide open for Buell to march all the way to Nashville, and there the discussion ended for the night. By the next afternoon, it was largely academic, because Fort Henry had surrendered.

News of the fall of Fort Henry had reached Johnston's headquarters by the afternoon of the seventh, and the general called an immediate meeting. Attending was Johnston, Beauregard and Major General William J. Hardee, the commander of the troops in and around Bowling Green. Some sort of decision and a plan of action was now required, and the three discussed the possibilities. Beauregard argued, at least at first, for a concentration of as many troops as possible at Fort Donelson in hopes of defeating Grant there before he could be further reinforced. Again Johnston disagreed since that would mean stripping most of his troops from around Bowling Green and leaving the way to Nashville virtually open to an advance by Buell from Louisville. Johnston did agree, however, that Fort Donelson should be reinforced and offered Beauregard the chance to take command there, which he declined citing his ill health. The agreement that finally came out of the meeting, held in the ailing Beauregard's hotel room at the Covington House in Bowling Green would be criticized by many as "to little and too late." It agreed upon a change in the command structure, with Beauregard taking over command of the now isolated western part of the department. With the destruction of the Memphis & Charleston Railroad link over the Tennessee River, Beauregard would have to operate independently, at least until the army could be reunited somewhere farther south.

The most important decision to come out of the meeting, however, is summed up in this passage from the memorandum, written by Beauregard, signed by all three generals and sent to Richmond:

> Bowling Green, KY., February 7, 1862.
> [Memorandum.]
>
> At a meeting held to-day at my quarters (Covington House) by Generals Johnston, Hardee, and myself (Colonel Mackall being present part of the time) it was determined that, Fort Henry, on the Tennessee River, having fallen yesterday into the hands of the enemy, and Fort Donelson, on the Cumberland River, not being long tenable, preparations should at once be made for the removal of this army to Nashville, in rear of the Cumberland River, a strong point some miles below that city being fortified forthwith, to defend the river from the passage of gunboats and transports…
>
> G. T. Beauregard,
> General, C.S. Army.

Stripped of its nineteenth-century prose, it says that Johnston's army is going to abandon the state of Kentucky and form a new line somewhere south of the Cumberland River. Later in the memorandum, Beauregard also admitted that the great Confederate base at Columbus, Kentucky, was now outflanked and would also have to be evacuated. Fort Donelson is given up for lost. Having said that, however, Johnston still decides to reinforce the fort with the idea of it holding out until he can get his forces from Bowling Green across the river at Nashville. He is plagued with visions of Union gunboats coming up the Cumberland and trapping part or all of his army north of the river.

Fort Donelson has now become, in General Johnston's mind, a delaying action at best, hoping that the garrison can hold for a few days and then slip away and rejoin the rest of army. In the end, however, he will choose the worst of both worlds, keeping the fort's garrison too small to successfully resist Grant's army but too large to be able to escape when the time comes. Johnston will also create a command structure that will be a recipe for confusion and all but guarantee the fort's downfall. Over the next eight days, the command of Fort Donelson will change hands seven times.[54]

With General Tilghman's capture at Fort Henry, the command of Fort Donelson fell to Colonel Heiman, who had brought the survivors safely there. He filed a report, tried to organize the scattered units at the fort, sent out a few cavalry patrols and waited. Major Jeremy Gilmer, General Johnston's chief engineer, had also been at Fort Henry but escaped on foot and made his way to Fort Donelson by the afternoon of the seventh. Gilmer found about six thousand men there and immediately began putting together work parties to create an outer line of defenses some distance out from the fort itself and eventually extending south to cover the town of Dover.

Major Gilmer and Colonel Heiman had both seen Grant's army and understood that much more than a few guns on the river and an earthwork fort would be required if the Confederates were to stand any chance at all. For the next several days, trees and brush were cut to create obstacles and clear fields of fire, trenches and rifle pits were dug and artillery positions were prepared; something like a real defensive line soon began to take shape. Meanwhile, Grant's army sat at Fort Henry, twelve miles away, moving its massive amounts of supplies to dry ground, offloading reinforcements from the transports and trying to get ready to march. There was probably no way that Grant could have moved any sooner, but Major Gilmer and his workmen would make him pay dearly for the few extra days he gave them.

Chapter 13

The Main Event

U lysses S. Grant may not have known about Henry Halleck's political maneuvering for command of a new consolidated department, or of his efforts behind the scenes to get him replaced, but Grant understood his commander well enough to know that, even after the victory at Fort Henry, he could change his mind any time and bring everything to a halt. Unfortunately, Grant's initial hope to move on Fort Donelson on February 8 was quickly dashed by the rain and the logistical situation. Transports were constantly arriving with military stores and new regiments, sent along by General Halleck. He may have been searching for someone to replace Grant, but in the meantime, Halleck did his best to see that the expedition was supported. Whoever was leading it, he couldn't afford a defeat at this point.

In the days following the fall of Fort Henry, Grant's biggest enemy was not his nervous superior in St. Louis or the Confederate army twelve miles away—it was the Tennessee River. In a telegram to Halleck, Grant described his situation: "At present, we are perfectly locked in by high water and bad roads and prevented from acting offensively, as I should like to do. The banks are higher at the water's edge than farther back, leaving a wide margin of low land to bridge over before anything can be done inland."[55]

While Grant was struggling to get his men and matériel ashore, the Confederates at Fort Donelson were doing their best to get ready for him. Now that the situation was critical, they were trying to accomplish in a few days what had not been done in the preceding few months.

Colonel Adolphus Heiman was the senior officer of Fort Donelson after he brought the Fort Henry survivors in early on the morning of the seventh, but he knew that it was only temporary. He and Major Gilmer began the work on the outer line of defenses, but, in the early hours of the eighth, the first of four brigadier generals to command the fort arrived. General Bushrod Johnson came from Nashville, with a stop in Clarksville, and Colonel Heiman reverted to command of his old brigade, which included his favorite Irishmen, the Tenth Tennessee under Lieutenant Colonel McGavock. Bushrod Johnson concerned himself mostly with trying to organize the tons of supplies that were piled up near the landing at Dover, knowing that his replacement was already on the way.

General Gideon Pillow had resigned about the first of the year but had been brought back and, at the time of the fall of Fort Henry, was in command of the supply base at Clarksville, just upriver from Fort Donelson. When the decision was made to evacuate the army at Bowling Green back to Nashville,

General Simon Buckner's division, General Charles Clark's brigade and General John B. Floyd's brigade were all ordered to fall back through Clarksville, where they came under Pillow's jurisdiction. By the time the lead elements of these units began to arrive, Pillow had instituted a policy of forwarding all supplies and troops on down the river to Fort Donelson, which he did with these troops as well— without consulting their commanders. By February 9, Pillow had taken his own brigade and moved on to Fort Donelson, replacing Bushrod Johnson and becoming its third commander in about sixty hours.[56]

Brigadier General John B. Floyd. A former secretary of war and politician, Floyd was the senior of four Confederate brigadiers at Fort Donelson. Out of his depths as commander of the army, Floyd turned over command early on February 16 and fled to Nashville with most of his Virginia brigade. *Courtesy of the Library of Congress.*

The diversion of these troops did not sit well, especially with General Buckner, who arrived in

Clarksville a day or so later only to find that Gideon Pillow had hijacked his division. He and Pillow had known each other since Mexico, and they had some personal history, going back several years and involving some political differences. To Pillow, Buckner represented the proud West Point professional that he disliked intensely, and to Buckner, Pillow was a pretentious amateur and something of a pompous fool. Unfortunately for Buckner, Pillow's commission was senior to his by two months. Nevertheless, Buckner, with the support of General John B. Floyd, who outranked both Buckner and Pillow, departed Clarksville for Fort Donelson on the eleventh, with every intention of retrieving his division from Pillow's command.

As soon as General Pillow arrived, he inspected the work that Major Gilmer had begun on the outer line and ordered it to be continued. General Bushrod Johnson was now given command of the left wing of the outer defenses which, at the time, consisted of three brigades containing about ten regiments. More matériel and troops continued to arrive as quickly as the riverboats could make the trip from Clarksville, and General Pillow worked to bring order to the somewhat chaotic situation at the steamboat landing. Lack of wagons and storage in the little village of Dover meant that much of the matériel was simply piled up on the ground, and the same wet weather that was plaguing Grant and his army on the Tennessee was turning much of the area around Fort Donelson into mud as well.

Since the fall of Fort Henry, the new Federal ironclad gunboats had become an object of great concern to Confederate commanders. General A.S. Johnston even

Brigadier General Bushrod R. Johnson. The junior brigadier at Fort Donelson, Johnson fought in the Confederate left wing. Captured when the fort surrendered, Johnson and another officer walked away two days later and escaped. *Courtesy of the Library of Congress.*

ventured the opinion that the gunboats could take Fort Donelson by themselves, feeling that they were more or less invulnerable to ordinary artillery. Had Johnston known that of the four ironclads that attacked Fort Henry three were now docked at Cairo and St. Louis for repairs due to Confederate gunfire, he might have been more optimistic. Even so, the ironclads were now a force to be reckoned with, and that made the river batteries at Fort Donelson one of the most critical points on the battlefield.[57]

On February 11, Captain Ruben R. Ross brought his Maury Artillery company off the steamers from Clarksville and reported to General Pillow, ready for duty. Ross and his Tennesseans were sent to the left wing, under General Bushrod Johnson, but before they got settled in, word came that men were needed to man the heavy guns on the river. Ross had commanded the company for about a month, and he volunteered his men for the duty, handing over his light field guns to be used on the defensive line. Ross and his men were trained artillerists but had never worked the type of heavy guns in Fort Donelson's "water batteries," so they hurried to the fort and began practicing the new drill.

As the Federal gunboats would shortly discover, Fort Donelson was not Fort Henry. Instead of being situated in a virtual swamp, Fort Donelson's two "water batteries' were fifty to one hundred feet above the river on the side of a hill. They were in no danger of being flooded and had a much higher angle of fire, being able to threaten the wooden decks of the gunboats. Captain Ross and his men were immediately put to work:

> *Arriving there, Captain Dixon, commanding, assigned us to the columbiands [sic], consisting of a 32 caliber rifle and a 10-inch smooth bore. Two 32-pounder sea-coast howitzers were also placed in charge of this company.*
> *The remaining guns (32-pounders), eight in number, were under charge of Lieutenant Jacob Culbertson, Regular C.S. Army, who had already drilled three infantry companies (Captains Beaumont's, Bidwell's, and Graham's) to them, as I was informed. We were all placed under command of Captain Dixon. We drilled diligently that evening and had commenced again the following morning, when Lieutenant Beford suddenly informed me that the gunboats were coming, and we set to work to prepare for them.*[58]

The 10.0-inch Columbiad and the 6.5-inch rifle were the heaviest, longest-range guns in the battery, but they both had defective carriages that Captain Dixon was urgently trying to repair. There was actually an "upper water battery" and a "lower water battery," the upper battery being farther upstream by one hundred yards or so. It contained the two thirty-two-pound Carronades—short-range guns that Captain Ross called "sea coast howitzers"—but they were useless against the ironclads. The star of the upper water battery was the 6.5-inch (thirty-two-pound) rifled gun that, like the rifled gun at Fort Henry, was deadly out to almost three miles. This was the gun Captain Ross would command personally all through the battle.

The ten-inch Columbiad in the lower water battery was commanded by Lieutenant Bedford and was on the far left of the line of nine guns. The other eight guns in the lower water battery—thirty-two-pound smoothbores—were commanded by Captain Bidwell of the Thirtieth Tennessee (four guns) and Captain Beaumont of the Fiftieth Tennessee (four guns). Other officers included Captains Dixon, Shuster and Culberson. Overall, the water batteries were manned by about three hundred men.[59]

While the infantrymen worked on rifle pits and the artillerymen drilled at the water batteries, the Confederate cavalry at Fort Donelson was being consolidated. Up until now, it had operated in companies and other small units, but on the evening of February 10 and the morning of the eleventh, Lieutenant Colonel Nathan Bedford Forrest's Third Tennessee Cavalry was brought across the river. As the senior cavalryman present, Forrest was given command of all of the mounted units, which may have numbered eight hundred riders, and immediately began to patrol the roads to the west toward Fort Henry that same afternoon. Within three miles, he came upon a Federal patrol, which resulted in a sharp little running fight to within a few miles of Fort Henry and allowed Forrest to get a view of some of the Federal camps. Upon his return, he reported to General Pillow that Grant's army was ready to move.[60]

Colonel Forrest's observations were correct. The day before Forrest saw the Federal's advanced camps, General Grant did something that he would never do again—he called a meeting of his subordinate commanders to ask their advice as to the future movements of the army. In Grant's stateroom on the steamer *New Uncle Sam*, Generals C.F. Smith, John McClernand and Lew Wallace said their piece. Lew Wallace later remembered that, true to form, General Smith, the professional soldier, simply said, "There is every reason why we should move without the loss of a day." McClernand, ever the politician, then made a speech, laying out in detail his plan that, to no one's surprise, put him and his division in the forefront. Wallace, the last to speak, simply agreed that they should move on Fort Donelson as soon as possible.

Wallace later said that he also got the feeling that his and the other generals' opinions made little difference since Grant had already made

Lieutenant Colonel Nathan Bedford Forrest, commander of the cavalry at Fort Donelson. When told of the surrender, Forrest argued that the way was still clear for the army to escape but was not believed. Early on the morning of February 16, Forrest led about five hundred mounted men in escaping down the partially flooded River Road. *Courtesy of Douglas W. Bostick.*

up his mind. Later the same day (the tenth), the order went out to all units to be ready to move on the morning of the twelfth. By the eleventh, the road conditions had improved enough for General McClernand's division to move east about five miles so as to relieve the congestion and make the next day's start go smoother. It was these units that Forrest saw. In the middle of all of this, more boats arrived carrying a new brigade of six regiments commanded by Colonel John Thayer of the First Nebraska. Rather than have them march overland on already crowded roads, Grant just put them back on the boats and sent them around to the Cumberland to meet him there.[61] As Grant's Federal army was making all of the last-minute arrangements to march the next day, however, another little drama was playing out at Fort Donelson.

Once the decision had been made to pull back from Bowling Green, General Albert Sidney Johnston seemed to become fixated on directing that operation personally and delegating the command of Fort Donelson and the Cumberland River to a subordinate. He had four brigadier generals available for the job, and by February 9, two of them had already arrived at the fort. Bushrod Johnson had first taken command from Colonel Heiman. About eighteen hours later, Gideon Pillow had arrived from Clarksville, taken command from Johnson and, politician that he was, made a speech vowing to defend the place: "Our battle cry—Liberty or Death!" That's how matters stood on February 11, but back in Clarksville, the other two brigadier generals had different plans.

John B. Floyd was the senior of the four brigadier generals, and as such, the command of Fort Donelson and the other forces on the Cumberland River fell to him. Floyd was a Virginian and a former secretary of war under James Buchanan. Seeing what was coming, Floyd, in the last few years leading up to the war, shifted military matériel to Southern locations that then were taken over by the new Confederate states. Some suggested that this amounted to treason, so Floyd lived in fear of being captured and sent north for trial. Floyd was a civilian politician whose military background was totally administrative, and many thought that he was already out of his depth handling one or two thousand troops in the field. Floyd had come to Kentucky a few weeks earlier with five small regiments and now found himself in command of upward of fifteen thousand men. He felt a little overwhelmed, to say the least, and because of this, he would be easily influenced by both Simon Buckner and Gideon Pillow,

Floyd repeatedly ask General Johnston for some guidance for his new command—even begging Johnston to come to Clarksville and see the situation for himself—but he was essentially told that he was on his own. Albert Sidney Johnston had never laid eyes on either Fort Donelson or Fort Henry and had no intention of doing so at this late date. That being the case, Floyd and Buckner, meeting in Clarksville, formed their own plan, which didn't include giving their troops to Gideon Pillow to be trapped against the Cumberland River. They agreed to use Floyd's men and Buckner's division to operate south of the river near Cumberland City, where they thought they could attack Grant's supply lines and still keep their way open back to Nashville. The only problem was that Pillow had already carried those troops off to Donelson. It was therefore decided that Buckner would go to down the river and bring back his and Floyd's troops, leaving Pillow to hold Fort Donelson with the forces that were left and get them out the best way he could. An order to this effect was drawn up and signed by General Floyd, Pillow's new superior, and Buckner set off with it in his pocket, arriving at Fort Donelson on the evening of the eleventh.

Gideon Pillow was not happy to see the new orders, especially delivered by Simon Buckner, whom Pillow considered a junior officer and a personal enemy. He was not used to being outmaneuvered, and he had no intention of being made the sacrificial lamb, left at Fort Donelson with what he saw as only a token force. Always a lawyer at heart, he told Buckner that he would not obey the order to release the units until he had a chance to speak to Floyd in person. Leaving Buckner temporarily in charge (the third command change), Pillow started out early the next morning up the river to Clarksville to find Floyd and argue his case. Neither he nor Buckner knew that it was already too late.[62]

Chapter 14

Wednesday,
February 12, 1862

The First Day

Finally, Ulysses S. Grant had his army on the road. Two days prior, when he published the marching orders to his troops, he had also sent the *Carondelet*, the only City Class gunboat still on duty on the river, on ahead to the Cumberland to meet him. The City Class boats were so slow that when moving from place to place, especially when going upstream against the current, it was often faster for another steamer to tow them. On the way, *Carondelet's* captain, Commander Henry Walke, sent a message to Flag Officer Foote in Cairo when he stopped in Paducah for coal, letting his naval commander know what was going on:

> U.S. GUNBOAT CARONDELET,
> *Paducah, February 10*
>
> SIR: *I received instructions from General Grant this evening to proceed with this vessel to Fort Donelson, on the Cumberland River, to cooperate with our army in that vicinity. I expect to meet you before I reach there. The Alps will take me in tow. I will coal at Paducah. General Grant will send the Tyler, Lexington, and Conestoga after me.*[63]

Flag Officer Foote would follow Commander Walke within a day or so with three new City Class boats to replace the ones under repair. To do so, he had to strip the crews off the damaged boats to man the new ones, which caused an uproar among the men, but Foote would eventually arrive with the new boats as well as the three timber clads that had been with him at Fort Henry. Fort Donelson would see the largest concentration of naval power ever seen on the western waters up to that time. In addition to the gunboats, at least fifty-four other vessels were involved in the support of Grant's army at Fort Donelson.[64]

February 12 dawned sunny and unseasonably warm—fine weather for marching. Two roads led east from the Federal camps, the northern one called the Telegraph Road and the southern one the Ridge Road. General McClernand's division led off from its advanced position by 8:00 a.m., with one of his brigades on the Telegraph Road and the other two on the Ridge Road. They were followed by General Smith's three brigades on the Telegraph Road. Unknown to Grant at the time, Flag Officer Foote had left Paducah about four hours earlier with his gunboats and eleven transports carrying about six thousand fresh troops. Commander Walke in the *Carondelet* was up ahead, already nearing Fort Donelson and would be in the area when Grant arrived.

On this bright Wednesday morning, the troops marched out in high spirits. For those who had come in those first boat loads eight days ago, it was a relief to finally have a day without rain. For those who had come as reinforcements in the days after Fort Henry fell, this felt like the beginning of the first grand adventure of their lives. Unfortunately for some, it would also be their last. Since the troops had come by boat, there were few wagons available for "nonessentials," so most of the camp supplies had to be either left behind or loaded onto boats to be brought around to the Cumberland. As has been the case with armies throughout history, much of what was left behind or sent on ahead would not catch up with the men in time to be of any use.

The men marched with the bare necessities—what they could carry on their backs. One of those replacement regiments was the Fourteenth Iowa, and First Sergeant F.F. Kiner remembered the march:

> *About ten o'clock on the 12th, we took up our line of march for this fort. The day was beautiful and warm and the distance about fifteen miles. We took nothing with us but our blankets and haversacks, three days rations of crackers and boiled pork; our muskets and cartridge boxes with forty rounds of cartridges completed our load. On our journey we rested several times as we had not been used to marching we tired very easily.*[65]

About the time the first Federal soldiers were stepping off, Gideon Pillow was boarding a steamer at Dover, off to find General John B. Floyd and plead his case. Simon Buckner, now being the senior officer, was left in charge, but with instructions not to bring on any major confrontation. Later that morning, Buckner decided to send Colonel Forrest and his troopers out to monitor the Ridge Road. Within two miles of leaving the outer defenses, Forrest ran into the lead elements of General McClernand's division, and the Battle of Fort Donelson was on.

Except for a minor skirmish back in Kentucky, the Union army had not met Nathan Bedford Forrest yet, but they were about to get acquainted. Forrest was not a West Point–trained cavalryman but was instead an instinctive street fighter, and as such, he was unpredictable. Unlike many of the professionals he would have to work for, Forrest was also naturally aggressive. His first instinct in a fight was to attack, regardless of the odds. He knew that aggressiveness was intimidating and could strike fear into numerically superior forces. He would later become famous for his simple rules of combat: "Put the skeer on 'em and then keep up the skeer!" Sacramento had just been a dress rehearsal. At Fort Donelson, Forrest would begin to come into his own as one of the greatest natural soldiers and leaders of men either side produced. Historian Shelby Foote once referred to him as one of the two authentic geniuses produced by the Civil War—the other being Abraham Lincoln.

What Forrest first saw was a detachment from the Second Illinois Cavalry under Major Mudd, scouting in front of Colonel Oglesby's brigade of General McClernand's division, coming down the Ridge Road. Having a good position on a small ridgeline, Forrest dismounted two companies armed with breech-loading Maynard rifles and opened fire. Forrest's dismounted men caused Major Mudd to believe that he had encountered advanced infantry pickets. The two sides sparred for some time until General McClernand came up and ordered his men to move to the right and outflank the defenders. Forrest saw the move and countered with his own move in that direction, which he followed up with a mounted charge, led by Major D.C. Kelly, against the new Federal position along a ridgeline. The Yankees seemed to fall back under Kelly's men, but they were, in fact, only clearing the line of fire for a new line of infantry and an artillery battery, which opened on the Confederates and drove them back. At this point, a courier from General Buckner arrived ordering Forrest to fall back within the entrenchment, and the first encounter at Fort Donelson was over.[66]

With the withdrawal of Forrest's cavalry, the Federal troops moved down the road, closer to the Confederate outer defense line. General McClernand and his division formed the right of Grant's army, and they began stretching to the south, paralleling the Confederate line and trying to cover the avenues of escape. Colonel Richard Oglesby's brigade moved down Wynn's Ferry

Road, followed by Colonel William Morrison's smaller brigade, but it soon became apparent that there weren't nearly enough troops to cover the area. The terrain was crossed by a series of ridgelines and valleys. The Confederate outer defense line ran along a series of ridges, and as evening approached, the Union army began to settle in along the next ridgeline to the west. The Union line was broken in a few places, as was the opposing Confederate line, by small streams and "hollows" that ran at right angles to the ridges, and these gaps were covered by artillery on the nearby high ground.

In the early afternoon, as the Federal units were exploring their positions, heavy guns were heard firing on the river, and the Federal troops began to cheer, knowing that the gunboats were here. Commander Henry Walke had brought the *Carondelet* to an area a few miles below Fort Donelson just before noon and, in accordance with Grant's request, had then come just around the bend and thrown a few shells into the fort from long range. He hoped to get any enemy guns to reveal themselves by firing on him and to announce to Grant and the army that the navy had arrived.[67]

To the north, General C.F. Smith's division came down Telegraph Road, arrived in front of the Confederate right and began extending to the south. On this first day, Grant had about fifteen thousand men on the field. More were on the way, but for today and most of tomorrow, the Union and Confederate forces at Fort Donelson would stand roughly even, with a slight edge of one or two thousand to the Confederates. Grant's own estimates, however, were that he was outnumbered by at least five thousand, so he was happy to settle his army in with no intention of provoking any major engagements until his reinforcements arrived.

The Confederates were of the same mind. Gideon Pillow was now back in charge, having returned from Clarksville when he heard the artillery fire, and Simon Buckner was back with his old division and had taken charge of the Confederate right. Like it or not, Simon Buckner was stuck at Fort Donelson. Since the outer defensive line was not complete, digging all along the Confederate line continued through the night.

The Confederate command was just as convoluted as ever, with Pillow back in command at Fort Donelson but still supposedly taking orders from John B. Floyd, who was still at Clarksville and asking General Johnston for guidance. Now that Grant's army had arrived, Johnston finally ordered Floyd to take all the troops remaining at Clarksville, go to Fort Donelson and take charge personally. When he arrived, early on the morning of the thirteenth, the command of the fort would change for the fifth time in six days.[68]

As night fell, General Grant set up his headquarters in a house owned by a widow named Crisp. This one small house, with a shed attached, housed Grant and his staff. According to Dr. John H. Brinton, who accompanied Grant, the staff's entire luggage was contained in one satchel, which he carried. Dr. Brinton was also in charge of the liquor, which Grant was accused of abusing. The doctor says that one eight-ounce flask was the entire supply, and at Grant's orders, it was only to be dispensed by the doctor for medical purposes. The privileges of rank also meant that the rest of the staff slept where they could, but General Grant got the featherbed by the fire. Also at headquarters was a newcomer, Lieutenant Colonel James B. McPherson. He was listed as "Chief Engineer," but he was also a special representative of General Halleck, who had sent him to keep an eye on Grant and report on his behavior. In other words, McPherson was Henry Halleck's spy. Instead of confirming the rumors, however, McPherson asked to stay on with Grant and eventually became a major general and one of Grant's and then Sherman's favorite subordinates. James B. McPherson was killed outside Atlanta in 1864.[69]

Grant's featherbed and fireplace would have been fond dreams for most of the men on this first night. The day that had been so pleasant turned into a miserable night of rain and sleet and cold. Some of the new men had discarded their blankets and overcoats on the march over from Fort Henry, and many more were ordered to leave such extra weight behind in company areas as they went forward to the front line, not knowing whether or not they might have to go into a fight:

> *The night was very chilly and cold. Our boys had left their knapsacks two miles to the rear and were without blankets. Cold, hungry and disappointed, we shivered during that long, dreary night…It was our first experience, and we knew nothing about making ourselves comfortable. We learned better after a while and always carried our blankets with us…During the night it rained and turned very cold. We were forbidden to leave the lines, hence could not go back for our blankets…Wilber F. Crummer, 45th Illinois.[70]*

It was no better on the Confederate side:

> *The weather had been pleasant, but now a cold north wind began to blow, bringing rain and sleet. As we were forbidden to make fires lest we make our position a target for the enemy, we passed a most uncomfortable night… Louis Douglas Payne, 2nd Kentucky.[71]*

Chapter 15

Thursday,
February 13, 1862

The Second Day

After a miserable night of rain and sleet, Tennessee's weather turned again, and Thursday promised to be a pleasant day: "February 13th was equal to a June day in Iowa. The birds sang, the squirrels chirped, and the first beams of the sun touched the leafless branches of the beech trees and turned them to gold…B.F. Thomas, 14th Iowa."[72]

As the sun rose, the Federal commanders continued to adjust their lines, with General McClernand trying to stretch his already thin line farther to his right, and the rank and file of the two armies began to get acquainted. General Grant, however, had given orders that this maneuvering be done so as not to bring on a general engagement. His reinforcements had not yet arrived, and he didn't want one of his subordinates starting a fight before he was ready. With all the jockeying for position, the two lines were, in many places, within easy rifle shot, so sniping from both sides became almost a contest. Farm boys from Illinois and Iowa matched their marksmanship against other boys from Tennessee and Mississippi all along the line. For most of the troops on both sides, this was their first taste of actual combat, so there was a great curiosity about it all, with men from the rear pushing forward, afraid that they would miss the excitement: "Skirmish fighting was a new thing to us then, and very many of us would beg permission of the officers to go to the front, if only for a few moments, as we all wanted to get a view of Fort Donelson and the rebels…Charles F. Hubert, 50th Illinois."[73]

Once the sniping got underway, everybody wanted to try it. There was even a reporter who had come with Grant's army who later wrote that he tried his hand at the "target practice" until the returning rounds began to strike uncomfortably close. At one point, a special unit of Federal marksmen (the Fourteenth Missouri, called Birge's Sharpshooters) was hampering the work on some Confederate entrenchments, and General Pillow called on Colonel Forrest to bring two of his companies forward and silence them. During this action, Forrest is said to have borrowed a rifle and knocked a Federal sniper out of a tree at a range of six hundred yards.[74]

Just about daylight, a boat docked at Dover carrying General John B. Floyd and the first of several loads of Confederate reinforcements from Clarksville. With Floyd's arrival to take command personally, Gideon Pillow used his seniority to take over the left wing from Bushrod Johnson, but due to his strong personality, he would still have a great influence on the command decisions at Fort Donelson. Floyd was in over his head and he knew it. Having failed to get any clear direction from his superior, General Johnston, Floyd was very susceptible to the opinions of both Gideon Pillow, who had a powerful if reckless personality, and Simon Buckner, who had the professional credentials that Floyd lacked. To a large extent, Floyd left the actual running of the command to these two men.

As the riflemen continued to snipe at one another, the artillery began to feel out their opponents, too. All along the line, batteries fired on one another and on bodies of troops that happened to be caught in the open. At a longer range, some of the Federal cannon fire began to fall in the town of Dover, causing men just coming off the boats to take cover.

The field artillery weren't the only big guns in action, however. General Grant had sent word to Commander Walke to bring *Carondelet* back up the river and shell the fort again, saying that the army would be ready to take advantage of any diversion caused by his attack. In conjunction with the gunboat demonstration, Grant had asked General C.F. Smith, on the Federal left, to conduct a reconnaissance in force to feel for any weak spots in the Confederate line. Sometime after 9:00 a.m., Henry Walke in the *Carondelet* arrived on the scene, and by 10:00 a.m. Colonel Jacob Lauman, one of General Smith's brigade commanders, had the Twenty-fifth Indiana under Colonel James Veatch ready to go up the hillside in front of Smith's line to test the Confederate position. Both Walke and Veatch would have a difficult day.[75]

Commander Walke had thrown some shells into the area of the water batteries and the fort upon his arrival on the twelfth but got no reply and did no real damage. Today, in response to Grant's request to try and create a diversion, Walke and his sailors on the *Carondelet* went to work in earnest. By 10:00 a.m. they were in position at the bend in the river, a mile and a half or so downstream from the water batteries, and opened fire. Over the next hour or so they fired 139 shells at the batteries, but this time the two long-range Confederate guns came to life. The 10.0-inch Columbiad in the lower battery and Ruben Ross's 6.5-inch rifle in the upper battery were the only Rebel guns that had the range to reach the *Carondelet*. Their crews had never fired them in anger, but now they had their chance. At first they overshot the target, but gradually they began to get the range. Finally, a 128-pound solid shot from the Columbiad found the gunboat. In a modern metal ship, a shot like that would produce shrapnel, but underneath its iron armor, the *Carondelet* was still a wooden boat, so this one produced a shower of splinters: "It passed through our port casemate forward, glancing over our barricade at the boilers, and again over the steam drum, it struck and, bursting our steam heater, fell into the engine room without striking any person, although the splinters wounded slightly some half dozen of the crew."[76] After this hit, Commander Walke dropped back down the river to the anchorage, several miles below the fort.

As the *Carondelet* began to fire, a mile or so away, General Smith began his probe of the Confederate line on the ridge opposite Colonel Lauman's brigade. With skirmishers out on both flanks, Colonel Veatch led the Twenty-fifth Indiana down the hillside and prepared to climb up the other side. This was the Indiana men's first time in combat, and they were handled pretty roughly. On the top of the hill waiting for them was the Second Kentucky, part of the Confederate "Orphan Brigade"—men from Kentucky who couldn't go home to their Union-dominated state—commanded by Colonel Roger Hanson. Hanson's six hundred men were in rifle pits with logs along the top, so the Indiana boys had little to shoot at, but up the hillside they went, climbing through the fallen trees and brush that had been placed there to slow them down. To the right of the Twenty-fifth Indiana, the Seventh and Fourteenth Iowa began to advance as well.

On top of the ridge, Hanson's Kentuckians waited with strict instructions not to fire until the order was given:

> We were armed with old flintlock guns, loading with three small and one large ball, very deadly but not carrying far...Col. Hanson...sent this order to each of our captains: "Let no man fire until I give the word." It seemed as if the word would never come. The Yankees were almost upon us... Then we were allowed to turn our guns loose. We could see the enemy falling..."Keep it up!" cried our captains...and we did...Louis D. Payne, 2nd Kentucky.[77]

And it wasn't just the old flintlocks firing "buck and ball" that struck the Union men. To their right front, Captain Tom Porter's battery swept the valley and hillside with shell and canister. All of General Smith's regiments were soon pinned down in the fallen trees and underbrush:

> *The air seemed literally full of flying bullets…they screamed through the air above our heads and ploughed through our ranks…We returned fire as best we could but all the advantage was with the Rebels. They were behind breast works and were little exposed while we were in plain view…B.F. Thomas, 14th Iowa.*[78]

That was the end of General Smith's "reconnaissance." It took some of his men the rest of the day to get back behind the ridgeline, but he found out that the Confederates in his front were there in force and had an excellent defensive position.

Farther south, General McClernand's men also ran into some difficulty as they tried to stretch around toward the river. A Confederate strong point with a battery of guns was "annoying" them considerably. This was a position manned by Captain Frank Maney's battery and supported by Colonel Heiman's men, including the Irishmen of the Tenth Tennessee. McClernand would eventually commit four regiments trying to take the position, but they would have the same experience as Smith's men. Lieutenant Colonel McGavock remembered that the Illinois men's charge faltered "a few feet from our entrenchments," where they were "repulsed with a terrible loss." The Tenth Tennessee commander said that the encounter was just "ten or twenty minutes, but was terrible while it lasted." McGavock later said, "My regiment behaved nobly and it was as much as I could do to keep them in the pits, they were so anxious to get out and charge them."[79]

Both Smith's and McClernand's actions stretched Grant's idea of a "reconnaissance" more than he would have liked but, in the end, didn't result in a general engagement. A couple of things became obvious: the Confederates line was substantial, and McClernand did not have enough men to complete the investment all the way to the river. Troops would have to be shifted to his sector to help. Accordingly, Grant sent orders to his one general who had, so far, been left out of the fight.

Brigadier General Lew Wallace commanded a brigade under C.F. Smith at Fort Henry but had then been left there as a garrison when the rest of the army moved to Fort Donelson. A lawyer and politician from Indiana, Wallace was not happy to guard a waterlogged fort while others had the chance for glory and fame; so when Grant's orders came for him to bring most of his men on to Fort Donelson, he was overjoyed. Over the next three days, Wallace would be a key player in the battle.

Finally, Commander Walke and the *Carondelet* returned and continued their shelling of the water batteries through the afternoon, firing, in all, 184 rounds, only one of which did any significant damage. Near the end of the day, one of the *Carondelet's* shells hit one of the thirty-two-pounders in the lower water battery. It dismounted the gun and killed Captain Joseph Dixon, who was hit in the head by a flying bolt from the wrecked gun carriage.

As night came, there had been several lively and bloody skirmishes, but the positions of the two forces remained basically the same, with the Confederates digging in even deeper and the Federals extending their lines to invest the fort as well as the town of Dover. As the sun went down, both Confederates and Federals again faced a common enemy—the Tennessee winter.

The first night spent at Fort Donelson had been quite uncomfortable for both sides, but this second night would be simply brutal. In most places, the lines were so close together that no fires were allowed that could provide a mark for a sharpshooter or artillery piece. There were few blankets or overcoats in the lines on either side, so most of the men, having now been awake for at least thirty-six hours, would get little or no sleep again tonight. For the men on the exposed ridgelines, the north wind, rain and sleet was agony. The next morning, it would be twelve degrees, with three inches of snow on the ground:

> *Came the turn of Co B to watch the* [rifle] *pits at night, and I don't think in all my life I ever spent a more horrible night. It was so extremely cold that our clothes froze stiff upon us and it was almost impossible to keep the men on watch. They were so worn out that many of them dropped down and slept in the snow and water...Dabney S. Wier, 14th Tennessee.*[80]

By about midnight, Flag Officer Foote finally arrived at the landing four or five miles below Fort Donelson with his convoy—three more City Class gunboats, two timber clads and transports bringing several new regiments. Now that the navy was here, Grant hoped that the gunboats could bring things to a speedy conclusion. Having to mount an extended siege in this awful weather was not something that Grant looked forward to at all. Although Foote was not pleased to be rushed into action, Grant would meet with him early the next morning and ask that the gunboats reduce the fort and the water batteries as soon as possible.

Chapter 16

Friday,
February 14, 1862

The Third Day

As the sun came up along the ridgelines, Federal and Confederate soldiers began to shake off the light covering of snow, keep out of the bitter north wind, light small fires on the back side of the hills and try to make a little breakfast. At the landing down the river, the new Federal regiments began to file off the transports and march toward the front lines several miles away, and at Fort Henry, General Lew Wallace hurried to get his men ready to march east to Grant's headquarters for further orders. As the sun came up and the men began to stir, the snipers also began to work on both sides. Also, unknown to each other, both armies were making plans for significant operations today.

In the early hours of this frigid Valentine's Day, the Confederates' four brigadier generals met in Dover to go over their situation and decide what to do. Both sides had seriously overestimated the forces facing them, but it was clear that the Federal army was being strongly reinforced, while the last of Floyd's brigade that had arrived late on the thirteenth might be all the Confederates were likely to get, their strength currently standing at about seventeen thousand. Everyone agreed that they would have to cut their way out or be trapped. The plan was for Gideon Pillow to take the left wing, attack the Federal right and open the road to Charlotte and Nashville. General Buckner volunteered to be the army's rear guard with his division. Simon Buckner certainly had conflicting feelings at Fort Donelson. He was there almost against his will, having gone only to retrieve his division, and he certainly had more respect for the opposing commander, an old friend and West Point upperclassman, than for either of his own superiors.

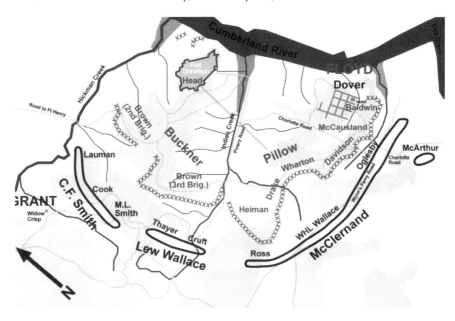

Action at Fort Donelson on February 14. *Courtesy of Hal Jespersen, www.posix.com/CW.*

For General Grant's part, he had a plan, too. For the last two days, General McClernand had been stretching his line to the right and now at least commanded the roads out of Dover. Even with some cavalry on his flank, however, he was still at least a quarter of a mile short of Lick Creek. Even so, Grant wanted him to be ready to sweep forward once the gunboats silenced the fort and water batteries and try to overrun some of the Rebel fortifications and possibly even take the town.

Having decided to break out of Grant's grip, the Confederate troops began to move to their jump-off position, but it went very slowly. It was about 1:00 p.m. before Pillow's force moved out from its position just south of the town, but after all of the preparation, it came to nothing. According to Colonel William E. Baldwin, whose brigade it was leading the advance: "We had proceeded not more than one-fourth of a mile, when General Pillow ordered a counter march, saying that it was too late in the day to accomplish anything; and we returned to our former position in the lines."[81]

Other witnesses said that the column was fired upon by Federal sharpshooters and that Pillow decided that they had been discovered and so ordered the men back. Whatever the reason, Floyd was livid when he heard what had happened, but by then it truly was too late in the day and so the breakout was postponed until the next morning.

Farther to the north, Lew Wallace and two regiments arrived at Grant's headquarters at the Crisp house just before noon. There his regiments were formed into a small brigade under Colonel Morgan L. Smith and sent to General C.F. Smith's division. General Wallace was then put in charge of a new Third Division made up of the regiments just off the boats under Colonel Thayer of the First Nebraska and sent to the center. On the way, they marched through some open ground and drew fire from some Confederate artillery but arrived at their assigned position in good order. Wallace then found why his assignment was so important. There was a hole almost a mile wide in the Union line between General Smith on the north and General McClernand on the south that he was supposed to fill. Wallace's orders were to hold the center but do nothing aggressive. As it turned out, the maneuvers of the infantry, North and South, were only incidental to the main event, which was just beginning on the river.

About 3:00 p.m., Flag Officer Foote brought his force around the bend in the Cumberland, about a mile and a half from the water batteries, and formed in line of battle. As at Fort Henry, he had the City Class boats in front in line abreast with the wooden gunboats farther back. Nearest the east bank was the *Carondelet*, a veteran of the Fort Henry fight and of the last two days at Fort Donelson, commanded by Commander Henry Walke. Next came the *Pittsburgh* under Commander Egbert Thompson, the *Louisville* under Commander Benjamin Dove and the flagship *Saint Louis*, another Fort Henry veteran, with Flag Officer Foote and captained by Lieutenant Leonard Paulding. Trailing behind at a distance were the wooden boats *Tyler* and *Conestoga*.

Had Foote known that the Confederates only had two long-range guns, the smart tactic might have been to stay at a distance and try to silence

Engraving of the gunboat attack on the water batteries at Fort Donelson, published in *Harper's Weekly*, March 15, 1862. *Author's Collection*.

the water batteries. His gunboats, however, did not have unlimited supplies of ammunition, and General Grant expected him to not only silence the water batteries but also run past them on to the landing at Dover to cut the Confederates off completely. Hanging back was not an option, but then driving past the batteries quickly wasn't either. His City Class boats, at full speed, could only advance against the Cumberland's swift current about as fast as a man could walk.

Captain Ruben Ross, commanding the 6.5-inch rifle, opened fire as soon as the first boat cleared the timber at the bend of the river, over a mile away, and the fight was on. Foote waited until he had closed to within a mile before he ordered his boats to fire, and the cannonade was continuous for the next hour or more. Each side would later insist that it was seriously outgunned, but in fact, the contest was relative even. Each City Class boat had three of its thirteen cannons firing from its front casement, which it tried to keep toward the enemy at all times. Turning broadside and using more of their guns could be inviting disaster, so the front line of boats had twelve heavy guns bearing on the enemy most of the time. The water batteries, at the time, had two long-range guns and seven operational thirty-two-pound smoothbore guns that joined the fight as the gunboats came within about four hundred yards, giving the water batteries nine guns for most of the time. The ten-inch Columbiad's carriage had been damaged again during the firing on the thirteenth so it could only be brought to bear on a small part of the river, but any boat that came into that area was in grave danger. The wooden Union boats also fired from long range but had little effect, except to damage some of their own ironclads with short rounds.

When the firing started down at the river, all of the other action on the battlefield stopped, and the soldiers on both sides tried to follow the action. The soldiers at the fort had a great view, and many others who could manage to get there watched from the hillsides. The Federals could not see the river, but the sound of the bombardment could be heard all over the field. One of the Confederate spectators was the cavalry commander Lieutenant Colonel Nathan Bedford Forrest, sitting his horse in a ravine near the river. Having never seen a battle of heavy artillery, he was awed by the four ironclad monsters slowly steaming up the river enveloped in smoke and flame. Turning to his second in command, Major David C. Kelly, a Methodist preacher, Forrest said, "Parson, for God's sake, pray. Nothing but God Almighty can save that fort!"[82]

In spite of Forrest's impression of impending doom, the fort and the batteries were actually taking very little real damage. A lot of dirt was

Cumberland River today, as seen from the lower water battery. The four City Class ironclads approached to within three hundred yards of the line of guns. The ten-inch Columbiad was on the far left of the line. *Author's Collection.*

being moved, but no one was being hurt, and the closer the gunboats came, the more they tended to overshoot the water batteries sitting fifty to one hundred feet above the level of the river. A good many shells were sailing overhead and bursting near the fort or somewhere farther inland. When the boats were about a quarter of a mile away, a priming wire was jammed in the 6.5-inch rifle, putting it temporality out of commission, but then the Confederate thirty-two-pounders opened up and the gunboat's situation became much worse. Anything inside about four hundred yards was point-blank range for the thirty-two-pounders, and all seven of them opened up at once. The crews—infantry men turned brand-new artillerymen—worked with a calmness and precision that no one would have expected and begin to shoot the supposedly invulnerable Union ironclads to pieces. There was the occasional massive hit by the Columbiad or the rifle, but most of the damage was done at close range by the seven thirty-two-pounders, which fired more than three hundred rounds between them.

The first to go was the *Louisville*. It was riddled with shots that almost burst its boiler, passed the entire length of the boat and finally shot away its steering gear so that it fell out of line and began to drift back down the river. The flagship *Saint Louis* came next. Being closest to the west bank, it received special attention, Foote later reporting that it was hit fifty-nine times. One of the shots went through the pilothouse, killing the pilot and wounding Flag

Officer Foote, who then took the wheel himself. Before long, however, *Saint Louis*'s steering gear was shot away, too, and it joined *Louisville* in floating out of control back down the river.

By now, Captain Ross and his crew had managed to clear the vent on the 6.5-inch rifle and were back in the fight. A few shots later, however, a new round became lodged halfway down the barrel and couldn't be seated with the rammer. Firing the gun in that condition was almost certain to burst it, so some of the men went in search of a small log of the proper caliber. Finding one nearby, they mounted the parapet, exposing themselves to enemy fire, and finally seated the round to put the gun back in commission.

At the lower water battery, the thirty-two-pounder crews realized that they were winning and kept up the pressure. The commander of three of the guns, Captain B.G. Bidwell of the Thirtieth Tennessee, commended one of his gunners, Private John Frequa, in his official report: "At the highest gun in my battery he stood perfectly straight, calm, cool, and collected. I heard him say, 'Now, boys, see me take a chimney.' The chimney and flag both fell. He threw his cap in the air, shouting to them defiance. 'Come on, you cowardly scoundrels!'"[83]

At this point, the gunboats were all but finished. The last two, *Pittsburgh* and *Carondelet*, tried to join up and protect the two disabled boats, but they were holed below the waterline and taking on water themselves. The *Carondelet*,

The Cumberland River today, as seen from the upper water battery. Captain Ruben Ross's 6.5-inch rifled gun was in the center foreground. *Author's Collection.*

Engraving of Taylor's and McAllister's Batteries during the Battle of Fort Donelson, published in *Harper's Weekly*, March 15, 1862. *Author's Collection.*

riddled from bow to stern, was the last to withdraw, firing all the way. One of its sailors later received the Medal of Honor. Suddenly, it was quiet on the river, and the men in the lines behind the ridges wondered what had happened. The Federal troops didn't have to wonder long, though, because for almost two miles along the Confederate line a great cheer went up. The feared Union ironclads were not so invincible after all.

The repulse of the navy's gunboats was not in General Grant's plans. Now there would be no capture of the steamboat landing at Dover and no attack by McClernand's men on the right. Things would have to be rethought, with the idea of a prolonged siege becoming more likely. The Confederates had gotten a terrific morale boost, and the prospect of a quick victory for the Federal army was beginning to dim. For now, Grant would continue to strengthen his perimeter and, in the morning, find out how badly the navy had been hurt. Lew Wallace's new division had plugged the hole in the center, and late in the afternoon, John McArthur's brigade had been detached from C.F. Smith's division and sent to try and fill the gap on McClernand's right near Lick Creek.

Across the lines, the Confederate troops were still celebrating their victory over the gunboats, but the generals were having another meeting—at least three of them were. For some reason, Bushrod Johnson was not invited to this one. John Floyd was not so concerned that Grant would attack anytime soon but was certain that he was receiving a constant stream of fresh troops and getting stronger by the hour. If they were to have any chance of breaking out, Floyd believed that it had to be now. Gideon Pillow agreed and offered a plan that was basically the same as the one he had canceled that afternoon. He would sweep the Confederate left around and attack McClernand's forces, pushing them back to clear the Forge and Wynn's Ferry Roads or farther, if he could. Simon Buckner would move his division from the right to the center and hit the Yankees in the flank and rear as they fell back. Buckner's men would then hold the roads open and act as the rear guard as the rest of the army escaped toward Charlotte. Buckner's old position on the right opposite C.F. Smith would be held by a regiment brought out from the garrison at the fort. This seemed straightforward enough, and it was agreed to by all—in fact, though, the three generals each went away with slightly different ideas as to what the plan really was. Subordinate commanders were then briefed and left to make their arrangements.

The breakout was set to commence at dawn. Unfortunately, critical details such as the order of march out of the lines, what the troops should take and other things necessary for an efficient withdrawal were not part of the briefing to the brigade and regimental officers. As a consequence, most of them had either a confused or mistaken idea as to the objectives when they went into battle.

Chapter 17

Saturday, February 15, 1862

The Fourth Day

U lysses S. Grant was up early. He had an appointment to meet with Andrew Foote on his flagship and find out the condition of the gunboat fleet. Foote had been wounded in the ankle and arm during yesterday's battle on the river and so had ask that Grant come to him at the landing. As Grant and some of his staff left the Widow Crisp's house about sunrise, they could hear some small arms and artillery firing to the south, but this had happened every morning as the troops began to move around and thaw out from the frigid nights. Grant had left orders that all units should hold their positions and do nothing aggressive, so nothing was thought of it: "When I left the National line to visit Flag Officer Foote, I had no idea that there would be any engagement on land unless I brought it on myself…The enemy, however, had taken the initiative."[84]

What Grant heard was actually the beginning of the Confederate attack on John McClernand's division, and before he could get back onto the field, it would peel the right wing of his army back like opening a tin can.

Gideon Pillow might have been many things—arrogant, vain, rash and pompous—but the man was no coward. In a staff meeting, Pillow could be overbearing, verbose and boring, but on the battlefield, he could be inspiring. Today he seemed to be everywhere, rallying and personally leading his troops. This was the biggest battle of his life, and he was determined to win. At dawn, he led the men out, and Colonel William E. Baldwin's Mississippi and Tennessee regiments made the first contact.

Colonel Isaac Pugh's Forty-first Illinois of John McArthur's brigade had marched over from the army's left wing late yesterday afternoon. Arriving

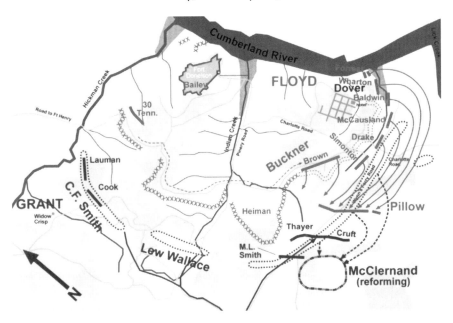

Action at Fort Donelson on the morning of February 15. *Courtesy of Hal Jespersen, www.posix.com/CW.*

after dark, McArthur wasn't really sure what was expected of him or even exactly where he was. As it happened, the Forty-first Illinois, along with the rest of the brigade, was camped on a rise locally known as Dudley's Hill, and Colonel Pugh and his men were just beginning to stir after another frigid night when they saw Rebels approaching and had the dubious honor of taking the first blow. Before the day was over, Colonel John McArthur's brigade would suffer about 27 percent casualties. Colonel Richard Oglesby's brigade, which McArthur had been sent to reinforce, was camped to McArthur's left and slightly to the rear and was soon engaged as well as more and more Confederate regiments arrived.

For most of these men, on both sides, this was the first taste of real combat. In the vernacular of the Civil War soldier, these men were about to "see the elephant" for the first time, and the view would be decidedly grim. The famous Rebel yell was heard by many for the first time, but the boys from Illinois stood their ground and gave as good as they got for a while until they were out flanked and had to fall back to a new position. Gideon Pillow came out with fourteen regiments, and their weight began to tell. After an hour, Colonel Oglesby's brigade was giving ground, and Colonel McArthur's was falling back to keep from being encircled. Forrest's cavalry, on the Confederate left, was finally breaking out of the timber and swampy ground around Lick Creek and sweeping around the Federal right flank, looking for opportunities. By now, General McClernand's position was deteriorating. He sent a rider to Grant's headquarters requesting assistance from the other commands, but General Grant was not available and nobody else would take responsibility for changing the standing orders.

As the Confederates continued to push back his units, General McClernand turned to General Lew Wallace and his new division for help. When the first messenger from McClernand arrived, asking for troops, Wallace refused. He had only been a division commander for about eighteen hours and was not anxious to violate his orders. Everything Wallace heard and saw from McClernand's direction, however, convinced him that something serious was happening. After another messenger came, declaring that their flank had been turned and that the division was on the verge of collapse, Wallace detached a brigade under Colonel Charles Cruft to go to their aid. After getting lost along the way, it arrived on the Federal right in time to support units from McArthur and Oglesby who were almost out of ammunition. These units fell back through Cruft's brigade to regroup and resupply.

This being the first major battle for most of the men and commanders on both sides, there were mistakes made and lessons learned, and one had to do with ammunition. The Civil War rifled musket was not a rapid-fire weapon. Soldiers in combat—especially rookies, like almost everyone at Fort Donelson—would do well to get off two rounds a minutes, so a soldier's standard combat load of forty cartridges was generally sufficient for normal operations. By now, though, the battle on the Federal right had been going on for three hours, and most of the troops' cartridge boxes were empty, and the men were now fighting with ammunition taken from the dead and wounded. Neither army had developed a good system for resupplying units in combat, so whole regiments were falling back in search of ordnance wagons.

Gideon Pillow and the main Confederate assault were slowly but surely rolling up the Federal line, but General Buckner's part in the plan wasn't going so well. To begin with, he was late arriving in the center because the unit that was to take his place on the far Confederate right was late getting there. It was about an hour after the first attack before Buckner's entire division was in position. The ground in front of them was on General McClernand's far left and was held by Colonel W.H.L. Wallace and his brigade, who were lined up along Wynn's Ferry Road. In front of Buckner's position was a battery of Union artillery commanded by Captain Edward McAllister that brought his position under fire. Buckner called in his own artillery support to silence

Saturday, February 15, 1862

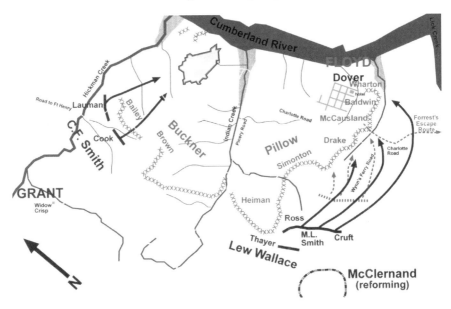

Action at Fort Donelson on the afternoon of February 15. *Courtesy of Hal Jespersen, www.posix. com/CW.*

the enemy fire and then, at about 9:00 a.m., sent three regiments across the hollow in his front to capture the battery and the high ground.

The Fourteenth Mississippi was deployed as skirmishers and was followed by the Third and Eighteenth Tennessee. As they crossed the small valley, the one Union battery became three, with Dresser's and Taylor's cannons joining McAllister's in sweeping the ground in front of them with grape and canister. The other two regiments fell back, but the Third Tennessee held on for an hour, almost reaching one of the batteries before finally falling back as well.

Even though it had beaten back Buckner's first attack, W.H.L. Wallace's brigade was still being squeezed from two directions. On his right, the Confederates were pushing Richard Oglesby's men back. Colonel John A. Logan's Thirty-first Illinois, on the left of Oglesby's line, had fought like veterans all morning but had finally run out of ammunition. Their place was taken by Lieutenant Colonel Thomas Ransom's Eleventh Illinois, of Wallace's brigade, but in the process Colonel Logan was seriously wounded and carried from the field. Lieutenant Colonel Ransom's gallant gesture soon worked to his disadvantage when he was left unsupported by Colonel Wallace's withdrawal a short time later, and his regiment scattered by Confederate pressure in his front and a charge by Forrest's cavalry on his flank. A short time later, Forrest would lead another attack that captured

<label>119</label>

McAllister's battery. Forrest, like Pillow, seemed to be everywhere and seemed to lead a charmed life. He had two horses shot from under him, and after the battle, his overcoat was found to have fifteen bullet marks.

Two hours after his initial probe, Buckner now attacked for the second time and, with help from the other advancing Confederate units, drove W.H.L. Wallace's brigade back and off the Wynn's Ferry Road. After six hours of fighting, the Confederates had driven the Federals right back onto themselves for almost two miles and were trying for more. The escape route for the army was now open, but Gideon Pillow saw a chance to actually smash Grant's army. John Floyd and Simon Buckner thought that the object was to get away, but Pillow thought that he could win.

Sometime after noon, General Lew Wallace, who had been following the sound of the battle all morning, began to see remnants of units coming down the Wynn's Ferry Road into his area, and it became obvious that this was a disaster in the making. Among the refugees was Colonel W.H.L. Wallace, leading four or five hundred men from his battered brigade, who advised General Lew Wallace (no relation) to form his men into line of battle because the Confederates were just over the hill and would be along shortly. Taking this excellent advice, General Wallace formed his nine regiments across Wynn's Ferry Road and waited. For the next hour, Wallace's men held their position. The Confederates attacked three times, but this time the Federal line did not waver or run out of ammunition, and finally, the Southern troops fell back into the timber. Lew Wallace, on his first full day as a division commander, had finally halted the disintegration of the Federal right wing.

It was now about 2:00 p.m., and something happened that changed everything. General Buckner and his men were finally in a position to hold open the escape route along the Wynn's Ferry and Forge Roads. They had come with their knapsacks and rations, expecting to act as rear guard and then march on to Nashville. Instead, they were amazed to see, off to their left, Confederate troops filing back toward the lines that they had left that morning. Feeling that, exhausted and with their ammunition almost gone, his troops could accomplish nothing more, Gideon Pillow, without consulting with John Floyd, his commander, ordered the men back into the lines they had left almost nine hours earlier, planning to have them gather their belongings and be ready to march out later that night. It seems that Pillow believed that the final decision to evacuate had not yet been made. Buckner and Floyd, however, did not share that opinion.

General John B. Floyd had been conspicuously absent most of the day, leaving the conduct of the battle to Pillow by default, but now, when he arrived to find most of the troops back in their original positions, he finally asserted himself: "In the name of God, General Pillow, what have we been fighting all day for? Certainly not to show our powers but solely to secure the Wynn's Ferry Road, and after securing it, you order it given up!"[85]

It had become clear that, whatever Floyd and Buckner thought they had decided the night before, Gideon Pillow had other ideas. However, as the three Confederate generals argued and General Buckner's men gave up their position and filed back into the line as well, something else was brewing that would make it all largely irrelevant.

About this time—early afternoon—the Federal commanding general finally arrived on the field. When Grant finished his meeting with Flag Officer Foote and arrived back on shore, an aide was waiting with news of the battle, and as fast as his horse could negotiate the frozen and slippery roads, Grant headed back. He arrived at the scene of Lew Wallace's stand on Wynn's Ferry Road to find Wallace and John McClernand conferring. However shaken Grant might have been, he resisted the impulse to fall back and "circle the wagons." Instead, he made an observation and two key decisions. Grant's observation was that the troops he saw who had fallen back from the Confederate onslaught weren't defeated—they were just leaderless. He rode among some of them shouting for them to refill their cartridge boxes and reform. Soon, other officers joined in the effort, and some order began to emerge out of the chaos. Next he ordered the roads retaken to prevent the escape of the Confederates in the night. This job he gave to General McClernand—who would later convince Lew Wallace to do it instead. Finally, he decided to order an attack on the Confederate right, convinced that in order to mount an attack with that much manpower on their left, they must have stripped their right of most of its troops and left it vulnerable. That job went to General C.F. Smith, who was already in position. Grant told an aide: "The one who attacks first now will be victorious, and the enemy will have to be in a hurry if he gets ahead of me."

General Grant found his West Point mentor sitting under a tree. General Smith and his men had been listening to the fight on the right all morning but could do nothing but wait. Sometime after 2:00 p.m., Grant arrived and explained the situation to his former teacher. "All has failed on the right. You must take Fort Donelson." General Smith, the consummate professional, simply looked at his former student and said, "I will do it!"

The five regiments of Colonel Jacob Lauman's brigade led the assault, with Colonel John Cook's brigade in support on their right. The Second Iowa was

Earthworks held by the Thirtieth Tennessee that were captured by General C.F. Smith's men on the afternoon of February 15. *Author's Collection.*

This picture was taken from the position held by Colonel Jacob Lauman's brigade of General C.F. Smith's division. On the afternoon of February 15, Lauman's men went down into the hollow in front of them and then attacked up the hillside across the way. The Thirtieth Tennessee held the opposite ridgeline with only three companies. *Author's Collection.*

literally just off the boat, having arrived yesterday, but it was selected to lead. What Colonel James Tuttle and his six hundred men thought of the honor isn't recorded. General Smith was brief: "Second Iowa," he said, "you must take the fort. Take the caps off your guns, fix bayonets, and I will lead you!" So began Charles Ferguson Smith's finest afternoon in his thirty-six years as a soldier.

To say that Smith's division had to come off its ridgeline, go down into a valley and then climb a hill on the other side to get to the enemy's line doesn't do justice to the terrain. One man said that it seemed that a rabbit could scarcely get through the brush and logs. Somehow, the Second Iowa did get through, and there with it, just as he had promised, was General Smith, mounted on his horse, a perfect target. As they struggled up the slope, Smith bellowed: "Damn you, gentlemen, I see skulkers. I'll have none here...Come on you volunteers! This is your chance. You volunteered to be killed and now you can be!"[86]

When they made it to the top, they found only three companies of the Thirtieth Tennessee, under Major James Turner. The rest of the Thirtieth Tennessee's 450 men were spread out trying to cover the line held yesterday by Buckner's entire 3,800-man division. The Second Iowa suffered almost 30 percent casualties climbing that hill, but when it got there, Turner's Confederates were overwhelmed and fled for their lives back toward the next ridgeline.

The only thing that saved the Thirtieth Tennessee, as well as the fort and the water batteries that were just over that last ridge, was the arrival, at just that moment, of Buckner's troops, coming back on the run after the aborted breakout attempt. With Smith's troops finally stopped, almost within sight of the fort, the Federals remained in the line of rifle pits for the night, while Buckner's men spent another cold night along that last ridgeline. Everybody assumed that the fight would continue the next morning.

Off to Smith's right, other Federal troops were also advancing. McClernand's division was so cut up by the morning's fighting that General Lew Wallace agreed to use his division to retake the roads, as ordered by Grant. Not long after Smith attacked to the north, Wallace went forward with ten regiments, back down the Wynn's Ferry Road. Most of the Confederates had retired to their trench line, but one brigade under Colonel Joseph Drake stayed out, trying to hold the road open. After a sharp engagement, Colonel Morgan Smith's brigade pushed the Rebels back toward their lines, and Wallace's men kept advancing. By nightfall, they had retaken most of the ground that they had lost that morning. Whether they had gone far enough to block the Forge Road and close off the Confederate's escape route completely is still debated to this day.

Chapter 18

Sunday,
February 16, 1862

The Last Day

That Saturday night in the Confederate camp, the generals argued about
Pillow's decision to bring the men back inside the entrenchments and
tried to decide what to do, but the common soldiers knew nothing about it.
They were hungry and bone weary, but they had beaten the Yankees that
day, and morale was higher than the generals had any right to expect. Even
though Floyd and Buckner were convinced that Pillow's actions went against
the plan they had agreed on and may have cost them the precious advantage
they had fought so hard to win, for a while it looked as if it might not be too
late. Early reconnaissance seemed to show the roads still open, so the men
were ordered to gather up their gear and form up to march out. As this was
happening, however, more scouts came in reporting that campfires had been
seen in the same area where the Yankees were camped the day before.

No one could agree, so Forrest was sent for and asked to send some of his
riders out. Forrest himself had been over that ground in the afternoon and
now took another look and said that he believed that the army could get out.
There was one road, nearest the river, that was certainly open, but it was also
flooded at one point for a couple of hundred yards. Scouts said that it was
passable for mounted men—with the water being about saddle skirt deep on
the horses—but questioned whether infantry could survive wading through
in the frigid temperatures.

In the end, General Buckner felt that either fighting their way out or wading
the flooded ford would mean sacrificing far too many of the men—he thought
they could lose three-fourths of the army. Pillow then asked if they could not

defend the line another day. Buckner thought not, replying that the Federals would attack his position on the right at first light, and given the condition of his men, he doubted that he could hold for half an hour. Once the Federals were over that last ridge, it was only a matter of time before the fort and the water batteries would be pounded into submission by Union artillery.

It was now after midnight, and the prospects for a breakout were looking worse with every new report. Finally, John B. Floyd said what everyone else was thinking: "Well, gentlemen, what is best now to be done?" Buckner said that he saw no alterative but surrender. Anything else, he thought, would just amount to a needless slaughter of brave men. Floyd agreed in principal but, given his morbid fear of captivity, would not allow himself to be captured. Only Pillow refused to agree, saying that he thought the others had misjudged the morale of the troops and that they could hold out another day—to what purpose, he didn't say. In any case, he also refused to surrender himself.

Having come to a decision, the details were worked out quickly. General Floyd would turn command over to General Pillow, who would, in turn, relinquish it to General Buckner, who would then open negotiations with General Grant. Both Floyd and Pillow would be allowed to escape on their own, with Floyd planning to take out his Virginia regiments on steamers that were due by dawn. In the middle of all this, Lieutenant Colonel Forrest came in and, finding that they were to be surrendered, stated emphatically that he believed the army could still get out. In any case, he said that he had made promises to look after his men and had not come there just to be surrendered. Forrest didn't change any of the generals' minds but instead was told that he was free to cut his way out and take as many as would go with him.

The formalities now were simple. According to a witness, Floyd said to General Pillow, "I turn the command over, sir," to which Pillow replied, "I pass it," to which General Buckner replied, "I assume it. Give me pen, ink, and paper and send for a bugler."[87]

Buckner composed a short note to be taken across the lines to General Grant and gave that task to Colonel John C. Brown, whose brigade faced C.F. Smith's division. The bearer of the note would be Major Nathaniel F. Cheairs, commanding the Third Tennessee since the wounding of its colonel earlier in the day. Cheairs and a bugler went to the lines and, after a considerable time in which the bugler blew every tune he knew, finally got the attention of men on the other side. Cheairs was taken to General Smith, who then took him to Grant's headquarters. Smith handed Grant the note and then warmed himself by the fire. Buckner's note read:

Major Nathaniel F. Cheairs, commander of the Third Tennessee following the wounding of its colonel. Early on the morning of February 16, Cheairs was selected to carry Brigadier General Buckner's message requesting terms for surrender across the lines to Grant and bring back his famous reply: "No terms but unconditional surrender." *Courtesy of Rippavilla Plantation.*

HEADQUARTERS,
Fort Donelson, February 16, 1862.

SIR: In consideration of all the circumstances governing the present situation of affairs at this station I propose to the commanding officers of the Federal forces the appointment of commissioners to agree upon terms of capitulation of the forces and post under my command, and in that view suggest an armistice until 12 o'clock to-day.

I am, sir, very respectfully, your obedient servant,
S.B. BUCKNER, Brigadier-General, C.S. Army.

After reading the note, Grant asked, "What answer shall I send to this, Gen. Smith?" According to a witness, the old soldier replied, "No terms to the damned rebels!" Grant laughed and then wrote his reply:

HEADQUARTERS ARMY IN THE FIELD,
Camp near Fort Donelson, February 16, 1862.

SIR: Yours of this date, proposing armistice and appointment of commissioners to settle terms of capitulation, is just received. No terms except unconditional and immediate surrender can be accepted. I propose to move immediately upon your works.

I am, sir, very respectfully, your obedient servant,
U.S. GRANT,
Brigadier-General, Commanding.

When Smith read it, he commented: "Same thing in smoother words."

Major Cheairs, as the messenger, returned to the Confederate lines and then brought back Buckner's reply:

HEADQUARTERS,
Dover, Tenn., February 16, 1862.

SIR: The distribution of the forces under my command incident to an unexpected change of commanders and the overwhelming force under your command compel me, notwithstanding the brilliant success of the Confederate army yesterday, to accept the ungenerous and unchivalrous terms which you propose.
I am, sir, your very obedient servant,
S.B. BUCKNER,
Brigadier-General, C.S. Army.

After delivery of Buckner's reply, Grant asked Major Cheairs how many troops were to be surrendered. Cheairs said that he had no idea of the total numbers but guessed seven or eight thousand. Grant, not believing him, replied that he had asked for the truth. Nat Cheairs, the proud Southern gentleman even in defeat, stood and began to take off his coat, saying that even as a prisoner he would not be called a liar. Grant quickly apologized, and the incident passed, but Cheairs, who lived to be ninety-six, never forgot it.[88]

For most of the almost fifty thousand men in and around Fort Donelson, the last ten days had been the most physically demanding and graphically violent of their lives, and now it was over, except that they didn't know it yet. The decision was made by three men in a small room, and the word only got out gradually. General Bushrod Johnson, the fourth-ranking man on the Confederate side, wasn't consulted and found out as he was continuing to prepare the men to try and escape.

As the word of the surrender filtered out to the troops, two brigadier generals made their getaways. Gideon Pillow was rowed across the Cumberland River in a small boat and eventually made his way to Nashville overland. John Floyd began to collect his old brigade—four Virginia regiments plus the Twentieth Mississippi—and commandeered two steamboats that had just docked at Dover. About four hundred new replacements who had arrived on the boats were marched off just in time to be surrendered, and Floyd began to ferry his Virginians across the river while the Twentieth Mississippi guarded the landing. Just as the last of the Virginians were boarded, word came that Federal gunboats were approaching, which turned out to be true, and Floyd cast off, leaving the Twentieth Mississippi stranded, condemned to a prison camp. Floyd and his Virginians didn't stop until they got to Nashville, and the boys from Mississippi never forgave him.

Nathan Bedford Forrest gathered all of his cavalrymen who would come, added some others riding artillery horses—five hundred or so in all—and made his way out the River Road and across Lick Creek without a gun being fired. He always maintained that most of the army could have gotten out that night if the generals had been willing to try.

General Lew Wallace was preparing his men for the dawn assault that he had been told to expect when Confederate officers appeared opposite his lines with a flag of truce. Wallace went to meet them and found General Bushrod Johnson, who gave him the news. Wallace then asked to be escorted into Dover, and when General Grant arrived sometime later, he found Wallace having breakfast with General Buckner and some other officers. In the meantime, Commander Benjamin Dove had docked the gunboat *Louisville* at the Dover landing and appeared at Buckner's headquarters as well. Today, however, unlike at Fort Henry, the army had beaten the navy. The first paragraph of the message sent that day to General Halleck in St. Louis was not only an announcement of victory but also a vindication of Grant himself:

FORT DONELSON, February 16, 1862.

GENERAL: I am pleased to announce to you the unconditional surrender this morning of Fort Donelson, with 12,000 to 15,000 prisoners, at least forty pieces of artillery, and a large amount of stores, horses, mules, and other public property…

I am, general, very respectfully, your obedient servant,
U.S. GRANT,
Brigadier General [89]

Sunday, February 16, 1862

All through the day, Confederates marched into Dover, stacked their arms and stood around in the mud with little or no shelter:

> *Crowds of confederates, very few of whom were in uniform, and who were unable to find shelter, stood in groups in the rain under guard of our men...A more pitiable collections of human beings was probably never seen. Dejected and exhausted, hungry, wet, and cold, they huddled together in the mud and rain...waiting for the rolls to be made out and rations issued...Very few had blankets or overcoats; some were without hats, their heads and shoulders wrapped in shawls and quilts as protection against the rain. Col. Charles Whittlesey, 20th Ohio.[90]*

Toward the end of the day, they began to be loaded on steamers for their trip into captivity.

Grant and his army had handled prisoners before, but never on this scale—nobody had. The actual numbers are still in dispute, but as Grant said in his message, somewhere between twelve thousand and fifteen thousand Confederates were captured at Fort Donelson. As Grant later wrote to his wife, this was certainly the largest single capture of enemy soldiers in the nation's history—easily half again as many as Cornwallis's army at Yorktown. The prisoners were being shipped north on transports, but the Federal authorities were pressed to find places for them. Most of the enlisted men went first to St. Louis and then on to other facilities like Camp Morton near Indianapolis, Camp Douglas near Chicago and Camp Butler near Springfield, as the Union army scrambled to find enough facilities. The field-grade officers went to Fort Warren in Boston, while most of the company-grade officers went to the new prison on Johnson's Island at Sandusky, Ohio.

Not all of the prisoners at Fort Donelson made it to POW camps, however. Security was so loose that quite a few simply walked away in the days following the surrender. One of those was General Bushrod Johnson, the second-ranking man captured. On February 18, after most of the other prisoners were gone, Johnson and Captain John Anderson of the Tenth Tennessee simply crossed the porous picket line and disappeared into the countryside of Stewart County, Tennessee.

All of Grant's division commanders and most of his brigade commanders (brigadier generals and colonels) would receive promotions, but his came first, which the others saw as only right. On February 19, President Abraham Lincoln presented Grant's name to the Senate for confirmation as a major general. The vote was unanimous. The obscure West Point graduate who had quit the army and then failed at civilian life had just won the first major victory of the Civil War for the Union. To a jubilant press, U.S. Grant had become "Unconditional Surrender" Grant. His short reply to General Buckner's first note had become famous, and he was now a national hero, with his name on the front page of every Northern newspaper. There were still difficult days ahead—and more conflicts with General Henry Halleck, who hated to be upstaged by anyone—but Grant had just won a new admirer, the president of the United States. Lincoln would later pay Grant one of the greatest compliments a politician could bestow on one of his generals: "He doesn't worry and bother me. He isn't shrieking for reinforcements all the time. He takes what troops we can safely give him…and does the best he can with what he has got…I can't spare this man, he fights."

Finally, an anonymous quote may capture Ulysses S. Grant's talent as a soldier and a leader of men as well as anything, coming as it does from an unknown Union soldier. Happening to see Grant calmly writing orders in the midst of an artillery barrage, one Northern country boy turned to his buddies and said, with a respect no combat soldier gives lightly: "Ulysses don't scare worth a damn!"

What Ulysses S. Grant and his men did on the Tennessee and Cumberland Rivers those ten days in February dictated the conduct of the war in most of the Western Theater for the next eighteen months. The Confederate army in the West would fight on for three more bloody, terrible years, but it would never completely recover from the disaster at Fort Donelson.

Epilogue

The campaign for control of the Tennessee and Cumberland Rivers, guarded by Fort Henry and Fort Donelson, was very early in the war in a theater of operations that hadn't yet gotten a lot of public attention. It was soon overshadowed by greater and bloodier battles, both in the West and in the East, so it is easy to dismiss it as a minor episode, but a look at the facts tells a different story.

The Fort Donelson campaign was the first great classroom of the war in the West. Many of the key figures in later actions in the theater, from private soldiers and noncommissioned and junior officers to regimental, brigade and division commanders, began to learn their trade in earnest amid the frozen swamps and snow- and sleet-covered ridgelines between the Tennessee and Cumberland Rivers those two weeks in February. The confusion, personal conflicts and cronyism evident in the Confederate chain of command, which was a major factor in the disaster at Fort Donelson, extended all the way to the president's office in Richmond and continued to be a problem throughout the war. So, too, would the political maneuvering in the upper ranks of the Union army by men like Henry Halleck and John McClernand, working for their own personal advancement.

While often considered a relatively minor action when compared to later western battles like Shiloh or Vicksburg or Chickamauga, the strategic impact of the fall of the two river forts was truly immense. In ten days, Grant forced Albert Sidney Johnston to abandon entirely the defensive line that he had held for five months. Johnston was forced to give up his portion of the state of Kentucky and a large part of middle Tennessee—an area of almost twenty thousand square miles. Seldom in military history has one battle yielded to the victor control of so much enemy territory. General Johnston and the Confederates were falling back as fast as they could. Within forty-eight hours of the fall of Fort Henry, the Union navy roamed the Tennessee River as far south as Florence, Alabama. Just over a week after the fall of Fort Donelson, two Union brigades, sent by Grant up the Cumberland River, walked into downtown Nashville and took possession of the Tennessee capital without a shot.

Fort Donelson was a vast schoolroom not just for the armies but for other organizations as well. In June 1861, the government had authorized the creation of the United States Sanitary Commission, a forerunner of today's Red Cross. After the battle, something over three thousand wounded men were at Fort Donelson, plus some twelve thousand or more prisoners who were virtually all "walking wounded" due to sickness and exposure. Fort Donelson became the Sanitary Commission's first big field exercise. It acquired a steamer from General Buell in Cincinnati, outfitted it with medical supplies, doctors and nurses and went to the battlefield. The exhausted military medical staff was overjoyed to see them, and they began treating patients and ferrying wounded men from both armies back to hospitals along the Ohio River:

> *The little town of Dover was full of sick and wounded...There was no adequate comfort of any kind; many were laid on the floor; most were entirely unprovided with a change of linen; and no one had any proper nourishment. What we carried with us was welcome beyond price. Rev. Robert Collyer, Sanitary Commission volunteer.*[91]

Partly because of its experience at Fort Donelson, the Sanitary Commission continued fitting out hospital boats that worked the western rivers for the rest of the war.

While most of the wounded had to trust the mercies of overworked doctors with limited supplies, a few were more fortunate. Colonel John A. Logan, of the Thirty-first Illinois, who was wounded during his regiment's last stand along the Wynn's Ferry Road, was blessed with a wife who was not only smart and brave but also very determined. Hundreds of relatives were crowding the streets of Cairo after the casualty lists were published, but civilians were not allowed on the army steamers going back and forth to Fort Donelson. Mary Logan had first heard that her husband had been killed, but when she found out that he was alive, she was determined to go to him. Being the wife of a former United States representative, she bypassed the army and went straight to Governor Yates of Illinois and Governor Morton of Indiana, whom she found in residence at Cairo. The governors had chartered private steamers to go and bring back their wounded citizens, and Mrs. Logan was soon offered passage. She arrived on the seventeenth to find her husband housed on Grant's headquarters boat:

> *I had not been so improvident as to go to Colonel Logan empty handed, but had clothing, delicacies, and many necessities…As I was the eldest of a family of thirteen, my education in caring for the sick and preparing the proper diets for invalids had not been neglected, and so I lost no time in finding the stewards and their kitchens…Mary S. Logan.[92]*

After tending to her husband, Mary and some friends worked among others of her husband's unit and attended her first battlefield burial, which she said was "unspeakably sad."

In addition to the thousands and thousands of men captured at Fort Donelson, the Union army found huge piles of food and supplies of all kinds. Most of it was out in the open, and much of it was ruined or destroyed. One Union officer said that he saw stray horses eating from bags of corn that had burst open, and sides of bacon that had been thrown in the street and used like paving stones. He said that about twenty thousand stands of small arms of all calibers were stacked along the streets and were then knocked over and run down by wagons and marching men until they formed a sort of corduroy road down to the docks.[93] Two days after the surrender, one Union soldier wrote home to his wife about what he saw:

> *We have won one of the greatest battles yet fought. We must have taken some 20 or 25 thousand of rebels and fire arms…to see the property distroyed is enough to make a poor man sick…if you only had the stuf destroyed you need not suffer while I am absent….I tell you we have to live herd…I had not eat somutch as would make four meals since I left home…dear wif, if I was to home I would stay ther for I have learnt a good lesson…W.H.H. Norris, 46th Illinois* [killed five weeks later at Shiloh].[94]

The Battle of Fort Donelson may seem like just a preliminary to the larger events that came as the war heated up, the armies got larger and the battles assumed more epic proportions, but at the time it was record breaking. Since prisoners were officially counted as casualties, the large amount of

Confederates captured meant that the four days at Fort Donelson officially produced the highest casualty count of any battle ever fought in North America up to that time and equaled about 80 percent of the total combat casualties suffered by the nation prior to the Civil War. Unfortunately, that distinction only lasted five weeks, until the Battle of Shiloh became the grim record holder. Ironically, most of the men captured at Fort Donelson were not lost to the Confederacy forever, like the dead and seriously wounded men would be. A few months later, both sides agreed to an exchange cartel, and by the fall of 1862, many of the men from Fort Donelson were back in Confederate uniforms and on the field, in exchange for Union prisoners held by the South.

The Fort Henry/Fort Donelson campaign had a wealth of lessons to teach, for those men perceptive enough to see them and honest enough to learn from them. A great many farm boys from Illinois, Indiana, Iowa, Ohio, Tennessee, Mississippi, Arkansas and Kentucky became men and soldiers on that frigid, hellish field. Politicians who fancied themselves soldiers learned what the price really was when the speeches were over and the killing began. A great many new officers learned what it meant to take care of your men on those frozen hillsides and along those windswept ridgelines. Whole regiments learned what war was really like as they followed men like Gideon Pillow and Nathan Bedford Forrest on the breakout…or fought for their lives with John McArthur…or held the line against repeated frontal assaults with Richard Oglesby or Lew Wallace…or followed brave, profane and magnificent old Charles Ferguson Smith up that hillside.

One of the men who began to come into his own at Fort Donelson was Nathan Bedford Forrest, who began building a legend for personal bravery and rewriting the books on cavalry warfare. The boy from rural Tennessee and Mississippi, who had little formal education and no military education at all, would later be studied by generations of warriors who would come after him, like George Patton and Erwin Rommel. Many of the concepts of modern mobile warfare that seem so revolutionary today have their roots with an old genius of a horse soldier who was one of the best instinctive warriors this country ever produced. Forrest knew nothing about modern technology or decision loops or most of the other things that they teach in military staff colleges today, but he could explain to the lowest private the philosophy of battle that made him a holy terror to anything in a blue uniform: "Get there first with the most men; put the skeer on 'em, and then keep up the skeer."

Another man who was willing to see the lessons that Fort Donelson had to teach was Ulysses S. Grant. He certainly made his share of mistakes during the campaign, but Grant and Andrew Foote laid the foundation for combined forces operations and provided an example of how the army and navy could work together to form a force that the other side simply could not match. Without the transport capability of the steamer fleet and the valor of Foote's sailors and the firepower of his gunboats, the campaign could not have happened the way it did, and U.S. Grant might today be just a footnote in history.

Appendix A

The Leaders

UNION

Henry Wager Halleck

After Fort Donelson, Halleck tried again, unsuccessfully, to get Grant fired. After Shiloh, Halleck took command himself, and after an excruciatingly slow advance upon Corinth, Mississippi, in which he allowed almost the entire Confederate army to escape, he was mercifully promoted out of the field and back to Washington, where he stayed for the rest of the war. Halleck remained in the army after the war and died in 1872.

Ulysses S. Grant

After being away from the field and surprised at Fort Donelson, he was again away from the field and surprised five weeks later at Shiloh. Like at Donelson, he was able to stabilize the situation and, by a strong counterattack the next day, drive the Confederates back to Corinth, Mississippi. Two years later, he commanded the entire Federal army, and four years after that he was president, serving eight years in the White House. In 1884, he was financially ruined in a swindle and was also told that he was dying of throat cancer. To provide for his family, he agreed to write his memoirs, and in less than a year, he produced the two-volume set, sometimes writing twenty to fifty pages a day while in almost constant pain. The final edits were finished five days before his death. They were published by Mark Twain and eventually earned his family almost $500,000.

John Alexander McClernand

Promoted to major general after Fort Donelson, McClernand served under Grant at Shiloh but continued to work his political connections to try and get his own command. Grant finally relieved him for insubordination, and he resigned from the army in 1864. He continued in the law and politics after the war and died in 1900.

Charles Ferguson Smith

Grant's old West Point mentor and commander of his left wing at Fort Donelson, Smith was promoted to major general and given command of the army when Grant was temporarily relieved by Halleck in March 1862. Smith moved the army to Pittsburgh Landing but injured his leg while jumping into a boat. Grant came back to command the army at the Battle of Shiloh while Smith lay sick. Infection set in, and Smith died at Savannah, Tennessee, on April 25, 1862, the day after his fifty-fifth birthday.

Lewis Wallace

Like Grant's other generals, Wallace was made a major general after Fort Donelson and served under Grant at Shiloh. After the war, Wallace remained active in politics and was appointed governor of the Territory of New Mexico in 1878. While there, he promised a pardon to Billy the Kid but failed to deliver and also published what became the bestselling American novel (*Ben Hur*) until *Gone with the Wind*. Wallace died in Indiana in 1905.

Andrew Hull Foote

Foote organized and commanded the river fleet that supported Grant's army in the campaign and personally commanded his gunboats in the Battles of Fort Henry and Fort Donelson, where he was wounded twice. His wounds forced Foote to turn over command of the river fleet after the fight at Island No. 10 in March 1862. Promoted to rear admiral, Andrew H. Foote died suddenly in New York City on June 26, 1863, on his way to take up command of the South Atlantic Blockading Squadron.

CONFEDERACY

Albert Sidney Johnston

After the fall of Fort Donelson, Johnston retreated all the way back to Corinth, Mississippi, where he reassembled the pieces of his army and attacked Grant's forces near Pittsburgh Landing on April 6, 1862. On that Sunday afternoon, while observing fighting near a peach orchard and a sunken road, later called the Hornet's Nest, Johnston was struck behind his right knee by a Minié ball that may have come from his own men. The bullet tore an artery, and in spite of having a tourniquet in his pocket, Johnston bled to death while his aides stood by. Johnston was never able to recover what was lost at Fort Donelson, but in the attempt he became—and still remains—the highest-ranking American soldier ever killed in combat.

John Buchanan Floyd

As the ranking officer at Fort Donelson, Floyd agreed to the surrender of the fort but then fled with most of his Virginia troops. He was relieved of his Confederate commission two weeks later but was then able to secure a major general's appointment in the Virginia Militia. Floyd died of ill health, said to have been brought on by prolonged exposure, in August 1863.

Gideon Johnson Pillow

Many believe that Pillow gave up the best chance for the Confederate army to escape at Fort Donelson when he brought the men back into the lines after their victory over Grant's right wing on the fourth day. He escaped rather than risk capture. Pillow never succeeded in recovering his reputation and had only one more command—a brigade at Stones River. After the war, he became a law partner of former Governor Isham Harris in Memphis and died of yellow fever in 1878. After Fort Donelson, Grant was asked by a Confederate officer if he was disappointed not to have captured General Pillow. "Oh," replied Grant, "if I had got him, I'd let him go again. He will do us more good commanding you fellows."

Simon Bolivar Buckner

After he surrendered Fort Donelson, General Buckner was sent to Fort Warren in Boston, where he spent over five months as a POW. After he was exchanged, he served through the rest of the war, ending up a lieutenant general in the Trans Mississippi Department. Buckner finally surrendered his troops in New Orleans, almost two months after General Lee, so becoming both the first and the penultimate Confederate general to surrender his army during the war.

Bushrod Rust Johnson

Johnson was one of two general officers who surrendered at Fort Donelson, but two days later, he simply walked away through the picket lines and returned to duty. He served throughout the war, being promoted to major general and finally surrendered with General Lee at Appomattox. After the war, he was the chancellor of the University of Nashville until his health failed. He retired to his farm near Brighton, Illinois, and died there in 1880.

Nathan Bedford Forrest

Lieutenant Colonel Forrest refused to surrender at Fort Donelson and escaped with about five hundred mounted men. During the next three and a half years, Forrest became a lieutenant general and, arguably, the finest cavalryman the country has ever produced. He surrendered at Gainsville, Alabama, one month after Lee. Forrest's famous comment to a reporter at the time was that he had killed thirty-one men in personal combat and had thirty horses shot from under him. He therefore considered himself "one horse ahead at the end," Forrest died in 1877. Maintaining the family fighting tradition, Forrest's great-grandson and namesake, Brigadier General Nathan Bedford Forrest III, was killed in a B-17 on a mission over Kiel, Germany, in 1943.[95]

OTHERS

The Tenth Tennessee, the Rebel Sons of Erin

This regiment was surrendered at Fort Donelson, exchanged a few months later and served till the end of the war. In 1863, Colonel Adolphus "Uncle Dolph" Heiman died of illness at Jackson, Mississippi, and Lieutenant

Colonel Randal "Randy Mac" McGavock was killed at Raymond, Mississippi. Of the 720 men who had mustered into the Confederate army at Fort Henry, exactly one was still on duty when they were surrendered in North Carolina in 1865.

Major Nathaniel Francis Cheairs

After taking over the Third Tennessee following the wounding of Lieutenant Colonel Thomas Gordon, Major Cheairs was selected to be the messenger to carry the surrender correspondence between Grant and Buckner. After two stints in Union prisons, Cheairs came back after the war to Rippavilla, his home in Maury County, Tennessee. Nat Cheairs lived to be ninety-six years old, but he never tired of telling the story of how he once challenged Ulysses S. Grant to a fistfight.

Appendix B

Order of Battle

CONFEDERATE

FORT DONELSON, ARMY OF CENTRAL KENTUCKY:
Brigadier General Bushrod Johnson, February 9
Brigadier General Gideon J. Pillow, February 9–13
Brigadier General John B. Floyd, February 13–16
Brigadier General Simon B. Buckner Sr., February 16

DIVISION	BRIGADE	REGIMENT AND OTHERS
Right Wing Brigadier General Simon Buckner Sr.	**2nd Brigade** (attached to 3rd Brigade)	2nd Kentucky (Col. Roger Hanson) 14th Mississippi (Maj. Washington Doss) 41st Tennessee (Col. Robert Farquharson)
	3rd Brigade Colonel John C. Brown	3rd Tennessee (Lt. Col. Thomas Gordon) 18th Tennessee (Col. Joseph Palmer) 32nd Tennessee (Col. Edmond Cook)
Left Wing Brigadier General Gideon J. Pillow	**1st Brigade** Colonel Adolphus Heiman	27th Alabama (Col. Adolphus Hughes) 10th Tennessee (Lt. Col. Randal McGavock)

Division	Brigade	Regiment and Others
		42nd Tennessee (Col. William Quarles)
		48th Tennessee (Col. William Voorhies)
		53rd Tennessee (Col. Alfred Abernathy)
	2nd Brigade Colonel Thomas J. Davidson Colonel John M. Simonton Colonel John Gregg	8th Kentucky (Lt. Col. Hylan Lyon) 1st Mississippi (Col. John Simonton) 23rd Mississippi (Lt. Col. Joseph Wells) 7th Texas (Col. John Gregg)
	3rd Brigade Colonel Joseph Drake	26th Alabama (Maj. John Garvin) 15th Arkansas (Col. James Gee) 4th Mississippi (Maj. Thomas Adaire)
	4th Brigade (Fort Donelson Garrison) Colonel John W. Head	30th Tennessee (Col. John Head) 49th Tennessee (Col. James Bailey) 50th Tennessee (Col. Cyrus Sugg) 1st Tennessee (Maj. Steven Colms) Stankiewicz's Battery (Lt. Peter Stankiewicz)
	5th Brigade Colonel Gabriel C. Wharton	51st Virginia Infantry (Lt. Col. James Massie) 56th Virginia Infantry (Col. Phillip Slaughter)
	6th Brigade Colonel John McCausland	20th Mississippi (Maj. William Brown) 36th Virginia Infantry (Lt. Col. Leigh Reid) 50th Virginia Infantry (Maj. Charles Thorburn)

Order of Battle

Division	Brigade	Regiment and Others
	7ᵗʰ Brigade Colonel William E. Baldwin	26ᵗʰ Mississippi (Col. Arthur Reynolds) 26ᵗʰ Tennessee (Col. John Lillard)
	Cavalry Brigade Lieutenant Colonel Nathan B. Forrest	3ʳᵈ Tennessee Cavalry (Lt. Col. Nathan Bedford Forrest) 9ᵗʰ Tennessee Cavalry (Lt. Col. George Gantt) 1ˢᵗ Kentucky Cavalry, Co. D (Cap. S.B. Williams) 1ˢᵗ Kentucky Cavalry, Co. G (Cap. M.D. Wilcox) 1ˢᵗ Kentucky Cavalry, Co. K (Cap. James Huey) Melton's Kentucky Cavalry (Cap. James Melton) 11ᵗʰ Tennessee Cavalry, Co. E (Cap. William Gordon) 11ᵗʰ Tennessee Cavalry, Co. F (Cap. William Martin)
	Artillery	Culbertson's Tennessee Battery (Cap. Jacob Culberson) French's Virginia Battery (Cap. David French) Graves's Kentucky Battery (Cap. Rice Graves) Green's Kentucky Battery (Cap. Henry Green) Guy's Virginia Battery (Cap. John Guy) Jackson's Virginia Battery (Cap. Thomas Jackson) Maney's Tennessee Battery (Cap. Frank Maney) Parker's Battery (Cap. A.H. Parker) Porter's Tennessee Battery (Cap. Thomas Porter) Ross's Tennessee Battery (Cap. Ruben Ross)

Appendix B

Union

District of Cairo:
Brigadier General Ulysses S. Grant
Chief of Staff Colonel Joseph Webster
Chief of Engineers Colonel James B. McPherson

Division	Brigade	Regiment and Others
1st Division	**1st Brigade**	8th Illinois
Brigadier General John A. McClernand	Colonel Richard J. Oglesby	18th Illinois
		29th Illinois
		30th Illinois
		31st Illinois
		2nd Illinois Light Artillery
		Battery D
		Battery L
		2nd Illinois Cavalry
		Company A
		Company B
		2nd U.S. Cavalry, Co. C
		4th U.S. Cavalry, Co. I
		Carmichael's Ill. Cavalry
		Dollins's Ill. Cavalry
		O'Hartnett's Ill. Cavalry
		Stewart's Ill. Cavalry
	2nd Brigade	11th Illinois
	Colonel William H.L. Wallace	20th Illinois
		45th Illinois
		48th Illinois
		1st Illinois Light Artillery
		Company B

Order of Battle

DIVISION	BRIGADE	REGIMENT AND OTHERS
		Company D
		4th Illinois Cavalry
	3rd Brigade	17th Illinois
	Colonel William R. Morrison	49th Illinois
	Colonel Leonard F. Ross	1st Missouri Artillery
		Battery H
		Battery K
2nd Division	**1st Brigade**	9th Illinois
Brigadier General Charles F. Smith	Colonel John McArthur	12th Illinois
		41st Illinois
	3rd Brigade	7th Illinois
	Colonel John Cook	50th Illinois
		52nd Illinois
		12th Iowa
		52nd Indiana
		13th Missouri
		1st Missouri Artillery, Battery D
	4th Brigade	2nd Iowa
	Colonel Jacob G. Lauman	7th Iowa
		14th Iowa
		25th Indiana
		14th Missouri Sharpshooters
	5th Brigade	11th Indiana
	Colonel Morgan L. Smith	8th Missouri

DIVISION	BRIGADE	REGIMENT AND OTHERS
3rd Division Brigadier General Lew Wallace	**1st Brigade** Colonel Charles Cruft	31st Indiana 44th Indiana 17th Kentucky 25th Kentucky
	2nd Brigade (attached to 3rd Brigade)	46th Illinois 57th Illinois 58th Illinois 20th Ohio
	3rd Brigade Colonel John Thayer	1st Nebraska 58th Ohio 68th Ohio 76th Ohio
	Unattached	1st IL Lt. Artillery, Battery A 32nd Illinois, Co. A

WESTERN FLOTILLA:

Flag Officer
Andrew H. Foote

**City Class
Ironclad**

USS *St. Louis*, Lt. Leonard Paulding

USS *Carondelet*, Cmdr. Henry Walke

USS *Louisville*, Cmdr. Benjamin M. Dove

USS *Pittsburgh*, Lt. Egbert Thompson

Timber Clad

USS *Tyler*, Lt. Cmdr. William Gwin

USS *Conestoga*, Lt. Cmdr. Seth L. Phelps

USS *Lexington*, Lt. James W. Shirk

Notes

PROLOGUE

1. Shelby Foote, *The Civil War: A Narrative*, vol. 1 (New York: Random House, 1958), 169.
2. Information on the careers of Ulysses S. Grant and Albert S. Johnston are available from many sources. Of particular help to the author were Charles P. Roland, *Albert Sidney Johnston: Soldier of Three Republics* (Lexington: University Press of Kentucky, 2001), Geoffrey Perret, *Ulysses S. Grant: Soldier & President* (New York: Random House, 1997) and Foote's *Civil War*.

CHAPTER 1

3. Benjamin Franklin Cooling, *Forts Henry and Donelson: The Key to the Confederate Heartland* (Knoxville: University of Tennessee Press, 1987), 4.
4. Kendell D. Gott, *Where the South Lost the War* (Mechanicsburg, PA: Stackpole Books, 2003), 3–4.
5. Ibid., 4.
6. Ibid., 5.
7. Ibid., 16–18; Cooling, *Forts Henry and Donelson*, chapter 4.

CHAPTER 2

8. Men like Braxton Bragg, Henry Halleck, George McClellan, William Rosecrans— almost a dozen all told. Perret, *Ulysses S. Grant*, 106.
9. The information on Ulysses S. Grant's early career and his reentry into the army at the beginning of the war is available from many sources. Especially helpful to the author were Grant's own memoirs, first published shortly after his death in 1885, and Geoffrey Perret's biography cited earlier.

CHAPTER 3

10. Foote, *Civil War*, vol. 1, 169.
11. The information on Albert Sidney Johnston comes primarily from Charles P. Roland's biography of Johnston, *Soldier of Three Republics*, cited above, 238–61.

CHAPTER 4

12. Gott, *Where the South Lost the War*, 49.
13. The information about Adolphus Heiman, Randal McGavock and their merry band of Irishmen, including the story of Tim and Paddy, comes from Ed Gleeson, *Rebel Sons of Erin* (Indianapolis: Guild Press of Indiana, 1993), 1–20.

CHAPTER 5

14. Commander Rogers's orders, reprimand and correspondence can be found in *The War of the Rebellion: A Compilation of the Official Records of the Union and Confederate Navies* (Washington, D.C.: Government Printing Office, 1908), series 1, vol. 22, 280–85. This work is hereafter referred to as OR-N. All references are from series 1, vol. 22.
15. The details about the conversion of the steamboats and the construction of the new ironclads comes from Gott, *Where the South Lost the War*, 23–28.
16. Captain Foote's orders are from OR-N, 307.
17. Commander Henry Walke would go on to command the gunboat *Carondelet* at Forts Henry and Donelson.

CHAPTER 6

18. John C. Waugh, *The Class of 1846* (New York: Ballantine Books, 1994), 246–47.
19. Lee Kennett, *Sherman: A Soldier's Life* (New York: Perennial [Harper Collins], 2002), 127–30.
20. Roland, *Albert Sidney Johnston*, 262–65.
21. Kennett, *Sherman: A Soldier's Life*, 133.
22. Letter of Private Burton Warfield, Second Battalion, Tennessee Cavalry, in James R. Knight, *Letters to Anna* (Nashville, TN: Cold Tree Press, 2007), 16.
23. Foote, *Civil War*, vol. 1, 148.

CHAPTER 7

24. Nathaniel Cheairs Hughes Jr., *The Battle of Belmont* (Chapel Hill: University of North Carolina Press, 1991), 10.
25. Ibid., 18–19.
26. Benjamin Franklin Cooling, *Grant's Lieutenants*, ed. Stevern E. Woodworth (Lawrence, KS: University Press of Kansas, 2001), 44–45. There seems to be some question

as to whether Smith, when given command of the troops at Paducah, was Grant's subordinate or a peer, reporting directly to General Fremont, as Cooling states in this reference. Grant, in his own autobiography, seems to agree, saying that Smith's "small district" was added to his jurisdiction only after Halleck's arrival. Only a few pages earlier, however, Grant, in his discussion of the Battle of Belmont says that he ordered Smith to send troops from Paducah as a diversion, suggesting that he also commanded Smith prior to Halleck's arrival. In the author's opinion, the correspondence in the *Official Records* indicates that Smith's was indeed an independent command at the time of the Battle of Belmont and only came under Grant's direct orders later.

27. My brief account of the Battle of Belmont comes mainly from Nathaniel Cheairs Hughes Jr.'s *Battle of Belmont*, cited above.

CHAPTER 8

28. Letter by Gustavus A. Henry to General Leonidas Polk, October 17, 1861, *The War of the Rebellion: A Compilation of the Official Records of the Union and Confederate Armies*, 128 vols. (Washington, D.C.: Government Printing Office, 1880–1901), series 1, vol. 4, 458.

29. General Smith's report, OR-N, 872; Colonel Heiman's report, OR, vol. 4, 461.

30. OR, vol. 4, 560.

31. OR, vol. 7, 731.

32. Gleeson, *Rebel Sons of Erin*, 33–34.

33. Thomas Jordan and J.P. Pryor, *The Campaigns of General Nathan Bedford Forrest* (New York: Da Capo Press, 1996), 17–57.

CHAPTER 9

34. It probably did not help matters that instead of Halleck's 1846 work Grant preferred, as a tactics manual, the 1855 book written by William J. Hardee, now a major general in the Confederate army. Perret, *Ulysses S. Grant*, 130.

35. Perret, *Ulysses S. Grant*, 154.

36. McClernand's report of his demonstration east of Columbus, OR, vol. 7, 68ff; Lieutenant Shirk's report of General Smith's reconnaissance, OR-N, 520ff.

37. Jack Hurst, *Men of Fire* (New York: Basic Books, 2007), 100.

38. Gott, *Where the South Lost the War*, 65.

39. Gleeson, *Rebel Sons of Erin*, 40.

CHAPTER 10

40. Chapter title refers to letter from Major General Henry W. Halleck to Brigadier General U.S. Grant, January 30, 1862. OR, vol. 7, 121. As of November 28, 1861, Captain Andrew H. Foote was promoted to flag officer rank, placing him at the level of a peer with both General Grant and General C.F. Smith (what today would be classified as O-7), although both Smith and Foote still operated under Grant's orders as the senior commander, OR-N, 444.

41. Grant's first letter to Halleck, OR, vol. 7, 121; Foote's message to Halleck, OR-N, 524.
42. Halleck's messages to Grant, OR, vol. 7, 121–22.
43. Perret, *Ulysses S. Grant*, 160.
44. Gott, *Where the South Lost the War*, 79–83. There is still some question as to when the initial landing of the First Division took place. Gott, in this reference, maintains that it was early on the morning of the third, while B.F. Cooling's *Forts Henry and Donelson* (page 92) says that it was twenty-four hours later, on the fourth. A.H. Foote, in his report in the naval OR-N, says that he was in Paducah on the third and was still waiting for the transports to come up from Cairo (Foote to Gideon Welles, OR-N, 534). If Foote is correct, the landings could not have taken place on the third. Colonel Adolphus Heiman, in command of Fort Henry, says that his scouts saw the approach of the gunboats, escorting the transports, and sent up signal rockets at 4:30 a.m. on the fourth (OR, vol. 7, 149). Unless both Foote and Heiman are mistaken by an entire day, just before dawn on the fourth seems to be the correct time for the initial landing of McClernand's First Division below Fort Henry, and that is the timeline I have used.

Chapter 11

45. Colonel Heiman's report, OR, vol. 7, 148.
46. Foote says that the attack began at 12:30 p.m., while Tilghman, at the fort, says that the gunboats opened fire at 11:45 a.m.
47. Gott, *Where the South Lost the War*, 94–95.
48. Ibid., 100.
49. Ibid., 101.
50. Foote's report to Gideon Wells, OR-N, 539.
51. Grant's message to Henry Halleck, OR, vol. 7, 124.

Chapter 12

52. Special Order No. 3, OR-N, 537.
53. Phelps' Report, OR-N, 572ff.
54. The information on Beauregard's arrival, the meeting and the Confederate's reaction to the fall of Fort Henry comes from Gott, *Where the South Lost the War*, 120–24, and Cooling, *Forts Henry and Donelson*, 123–28. The full text of the three generals' memorandum, and other correspondence, is found in OR, vol. 7, 861ff.

Chapter 13

55. Gott, *Where the South Lost the War*, 126.
56. Ibid., 124–25.
57. A.S. Johnston, OR, vol. 7, 131.
58. Ruben R. Ross, OR, vol. 7, 397–98.

59. Gott, *Where the South Lost the War*, 180.

60. Jordan and Pryor, *Campaigns of General Nathan Bedford Forrest*, 56–57.

61. Hurst, *Men of Fire*, 175–76.

62. Gott, *Where the South Lost the War*, 133–34.

Chapter 14

63. OR-N, 584.

64. Gott, *Where the South Lost the War*, Appendix B, 289.

65. F.F. Kiner, *One Year's Soldiering* (Nabu Public Domain reprints) 28. A part of a Civil War infantryman's basic gear was his cartridge box—a leather pouch that hung by a strap on his right side. It was divided in half by a metal partition, and each side could hold twenty rolled paper cartridges. The forty rounds that Kiner mentions were therefore considered a basic combat load—one full cartridge box.

66. Forrest's report, OR, vol. 7, 383ff; report of Colonel Richard J. Oglesby, OR, vol. 7, 183.

67. Henry Walke's report, OR-N, 587–88.

68. The five command changes include the few hours that Simon Buckner was in charge while Pillow was en route to and from Clarksville. As of the morning of the thirteenth, the changes were: Colonel Heiman to Bushrod Johnson; Johnson to Pillow; Pillow to Buckner; Buckner back to Pillow; and Pillow to the arriving John Floyd. There would be two more.

69. John H. Brinton, *Personal Memoirs of John H. Brinton* (Carbondale: Southern Illinois University, 1996), 116, 180–81.

70. David R. Logsdon, *Eyewitness to the Battle of Fort Donelson* (Nashville, TN: Kettle Mills Press, 1998), 6.

71. Ibid., 7.

Chapter 15

72. Logsdon, *Eyewitness to the Battle of Fort Donelson*, 9.

73. Ibid.

74. Jordan and Pryor, *Campaigns of General Nathan Bedford Forrest*, 64.

75. Hurst, *Men of Fire*, 208–9.

76. Henry Walke report, OR-N, 588.

77. Logsdon, *Eyewitness to the Battle of Fort Donelson*, 13–14.

78. Ibid., 14.

79. Randal McGavock as quoted in Hurst, *Men of Fire*, 214; Gleeson, *Rebel Sons of Erin*, 98.

80. Logsdon, *Eyewitness to the Battle of Fort Donelson*, 19.

CHAPTER 16

81. Report of Colonel William E. Baldwin, OR, vol. 7, 338.
82. Hurst, *Men of Fire*, 225.
83. Captain B.G. Bidwell report, OR, vol. 7, 395.

CHAPTER 17

84. Ulysses S. Grant, *Personal Memoirs of U.S. Grant* (New York: Da Capo Press, 2001), 155–56.
85. Gott, *Where the South Lost the War*, 220.
86. Hurst, *Men of Fire*, 278–79.

CHAPTER 18

87. Hurst, *Men of Fire*, 297–98.
88. Grant and Buckner messages from OR, vol. 7, 160ff; Grant and Smith's conversation from Brinton, *Personal Memoirs*, 129–30; Major Nat Cheairs's experiences from Nathaniel Cheairs Hughes Jr., *I'll Sting if I Can: The Life and Prison Letters of Major N.F. Cheairs, CAS* (Signal Mountain, TN: Mountain Press, 1998), 52.
89. OR, vol. 7, 159.
90. Logsdon, *Eyewitness to the Battle of Fort Donelson*, 97.

EPILOGUE

91. Ibid., 110.
92. Ibid., 109–10.
93. Colonel Charles Whittlesey as quoted in Logsdon, *Eyewitness to the Battle of Fort Donelson*, 98.
94. Letter from William Henry Harrison Norris, Company I, Forty-sixth Illinois, to his wife, Ellen, February 18, 1862. Letter courtesy of Bob Rounds, in honor of Dale Glenwood Rounds and Clark Stuart Rounds.

APPENDIX A: THE LEADERS

95. Additional information about the leaders from Jack D. Welsh, *Medical Histories of Confederate Generals* (Kent, OH: Kent State University Press, 1995), as well as Welsh's *Medical History of Union Generals* (Kent, OH: Kent State University Press), 1996.

Index

About the Author

James R. Knight is a graduate of Harding University, 1967. He spent five years as a pilot in the United States Air Force, flying the C-130E, and thirty-one years as a pilot for Federal Express, flying the Dassault DA-20 Falcon, the Boeing 727 and the McDonnell Douglass DC-10.

In the early '90s, he began researching a historical incident in his hometown and published his first work, an article in the *Arkansas Historical Quarterly* in 1997. In 2003, Eakin Press published his biography of two Texas outlaws titled *Bonnie and Clyde: A 21st Century Update*. In 2007, he published the story and correspondence of a Confederate cavalryman from Tennessee titled *Letters to Anna*. This is his second work in The History Press's Sesquicentennial Series, having written *The Battle of Franklin* in 2009.

Courtesy of Judy Knight.

Knight retired from Federal Express in 2004 and lives in Franklin, Tennessee, where he works part time as a historical interpreter for the Battle of Franklin Trust. When not encouraging visitor at the Carter House to relive some moments of the Battle of Franklin, he sings on the worship team at church, collects historical documents and artifacts and occasionally drives around in his restored 1934 Ford V-8. He and his wife, Judy, and have three children and six grandchildren.

Visit us at
www.historypress.net